"Sharing your culture by cooking at home with your family and friends is so important. Furthermore, having a garden at home is such a great way to have a direct connection with the ingredients you are combining. Taking these homegrown items and manipulating them as little as possible to create fresh, authentic dishes is the best way to honor your heritage and culture. Getting back to the basics and really perfecting those family recipes are so crucial to carrying on tradition."

—Aarón Sánchez
chef/owner of Johnny Sánchez

"If you have seen Marcela on the Food Network or follow her on social media, you know, like I do, that this is a long-awaited cookbook. You have also probably witnessed the careful making, step by step, of her Casa Marcela, a place full of color, warmth, humor, and love for family, friends, and neighbors. A place with a gorgeous and unique style. A place with ridiculously delicious food, where past and present blend to show how tasty Mexican in America can be. With this book, Marcela, without any reservations, has swung the door wide open to her home and has wholeheartedly invited us in. You can't miss out!"

—Pati Jinich
chef, author, and PBS host of *Pati's Mexican Table*

CASA
Marcela

CASA Marcela

Recipes and Food Stories of My Life in the Californias

MARCELA VALLADOLID

Foreword by
GEOFFREY ZAKARIAN

Photography by
CORAL VON ZUMWALT

Houghton Mifflin Harcourt
Boston   New York
2017

For information about permission to
reproduce selections from this book, write
to trade.permissions@hmhco.com or to
Permissions, Houghton Mifflin Harcourt
Publishing Company, 3 Park Avenue,
19th Floor, New York, New York 10016.

www.hmhco.com

Library of Congress Cataloging-in-
Publication Data is available.

ISBN 978-0-544-80855-3 (paper over
board); 978-0-544-80857-7 (ebook)

Cover and book design by Shubhani Sarkar

Printed in China
TOP 10 9 8 7 6 5 4 3 2 1

Para
Felipe, Fausto, David, Kongo
y la pequeña que viene en camino . . . .
mi familia

CONTENTS

Foreword   ix

Acknowledgments   xi

Introduction   xiii

Small Bites
Botanas   1

Salads and Soups
Ensaladas y Sopas   45

Entrées
Platillos Fuertes   75

Sides
Guarniciones   123

Salsas
Salsas   137

Breakfast
Desayunos   159

Drinks
Bebidas   203

Desserts
Postres   219

Index   259

FOREWORD

First impressions are important. I knew this for a fact when I first got to know Marcela during the spring of 2013 when we were both auditioning for the Food Network show *The Kitchen*. We were both up for a cohost position, and we struck up a conversation about food and somehow got to talking about our experiences with French cooking and family and home cooking, and how we cooked for our children and family. I was struck by how naturally the information flowed from Marcela and how comfortable and enchanting her food experiences were. All her food and recipe experiences were totally from her family background, her stint at the Ritz Escoffier learning pastry, and what she was taught by her aunt Marcela, who had her own culinary school in Tijuana. It was then that I learned a good lesson about how we sometimes forget how important our family and its effect on our lives can be, and how lasting and incredibly deep and personal such homespun experiences are. You don't need to work as a professional chef for years on end to understand food and real cooking. I felt an immediate kinship with Marcela that has grown into a wonderful friendship and, thankfully, a lot of Food Network shows together, and it was all because of those first impressions.

Casa Marcela, her new cookbook, is another important impression. So I was so touched and honored when she asked me to write a foreword to this amazingly beautiful and deeply personal cookbook. Since this is my first ever foreword, I said I would be delighted, but only if I had all the recipes ahead of time in order to read each one of them to really understand her point of view as it relates to her blending of Mexican cuisine, of which I know very little, and classic French cuisine, which I fancy myself as pretty comfortable with. Yes, I have read all the recipes thoroughly, and quickly pronounced to my wife and three children that we will immediately learn how to cook real Mexican cuisine because we now have the best book on the subject that currently exists . . . I told you first impressions are important!

Marcela's food story tells itself through her love and devotion to her family and her dedication to growing most of everything she eats from her own garden. Her deeply rooted understanding and love of food, family, and nourishment in all forms is evident in every single recipe.

When reading through the book for the first time, I stopped midread and started making her *asado de tira*, or grilled beef strips, and then immediately prepared another shopping list for the amazing jalapeño roasted chicken and Mexican ramen . . . yes, Mexican ramen!! And the sweet potato enchiladas, coke-braised pork tacos, squash blossom quesadillas, and, I guarantee you, the best *aguachile* you've ever had. The recipes are simple to follow, remarkably delicious, and, for me, an eye-opening culinary learning experience. I did not know how much I did not know about this wonderful food culture and Marcela's unique take on its cuisine. The photos of the food and her presentation and style are simply too stunning to explain, so I will simply refrain and just say, wow!

I cherish our friendship and have so much respect for Marcela. She is a delightful and deeply soulful person. This book has so brightened my culinary horizons, and I am deeply grateful for Marcela for writing such a special, creative, and inspired cookbook that will have your family begging for more. If you've held off on diving into the flavors and colors of Mexican cuisine, you're so lucky, because Marcela Valladolid has created a wonderfully warm home that you will never want to leave. Get it, read it, drink it in, and go begin your new culinary journey, as I did.

Buen Provecho,

GEOFFREY ZAKARIAN
Iron Chef

ACKNOWLEDGMENTS

I've always said you are only as good as the people you are smart enough to surround yourself with, and I must be some sort of genius because the small army that helped me put this book together surpassed all my expectations and then some. This is just a list with their social media handles so you can find them.

My team, my girls, my *Mexicanas*, aunts to my boys, my writers, my *familia*:
    Viviana Ley @vivianaley
    Marla Marquez @mmmarqz
    Valeria Linns @valerialm
    Isabella Martinez-Funcke @isabellamfuncke

My photographers:
    Coral von Zumwalt @coralvz
    Alyssa Gonzalez @alyssagtorres
    Isabella Martinez-Funcke @isabellamfuncke

The best prop stylist I've ever known:
    Robin Turk @robinturkstylist

My food stylist:
    Sandra Cordero @chefsandracordero

My glam squad:
    Lindsey Jones @lindseymaureenjones
    Lizette Prado @liphz.makeup
    Mirelle Hernandez @mimisskisss
    Gala Susana Navarrete @galasglamoroustogo

The Intimate Living Interiors designer extraordinaire who helped make this home a dream come true:
Kari Arendsen @kari_arendsen

Our friends that worked on flowers, table decor, rentals, and anything creative:
Erika Funcke and Isabella Martinez-Funcke @hijadetumadredecor
Melissa Strukel and Corbin Winters @powwowdesignstudio
Sarah Neal from Catalina Neal Floral and Design @catalinaneal
Ana Isabel Hermosillo @winygram

My PR team that has been with me since day one:
The Door @thedooronline

The most patient book editor in the history of book editors, from Houghton Mifflin Harcourt:
Justin Schwartz @justcooknyc

The woman and company who helped the garden that existed in my head for almost a decade become a reality:
Karen Contreras @urbanplantations

The people that make sure Casa Marcela is in pristine condition every day and who I very much consider my family after so many years:
María Guadalupe Morales, Luis Galo, Selene Llamas, María Fernanda Morales, Leticia Barrón, and Imelda Pérez

My friends and family for always supporting me and constantly encouraging me to keep going.

The loves of my life, Felipe, Fausto, David, Kongo, and the baby girl who's coming; thank you for giving my life purpose.

INTRODUCTION

When I walked into this house four years ago, I could neither afford it nor use all of it. It made no sense. Back then it was only my son, Fau, my thirteen-year-old one-eyed shih tzu, Yogo, and myself. If you added the three of us in weight, you barely made a full adult. We didn't need this house. In fact, both Fau and I like small spaces, and a house like this house seemed daunting and a little bit scary. So much work needed to be done. Even though the previous owner, Ms. Garcia, had done an impeccable job preserving the 1912 Chula Vista landmark, and we couldn't make any architectural changes, per my design aesthetic all the interiors needed to be redone. Plus, I barely had enough money in the bank to make the down payment, which would practically wipe me out, let alone remodel it. I was being considered for the cast of this new show on the Food Network, but we hadn't locked anything down. It would have been a really risky move for a single working mom who was determined to keep her kid in the same school that his cousins attended to purchase this home. Oh, but the house . . . I knew it made no sense, but I saw the *posadas*, I could smell the turkey in the dining room, and I envisioned the garden. I saw it, all of it. Not just for me and Fau, but all those years that I wouldn't hold a family gathering because my apartments were too small for my extended family. This dining room was the answer, and I knew I would never find another home like this in Chula Vista.

A few years prior, as a competitor on *The Apprentice: Martha Stewart* (remember that show?), I got to visit Martha's farm in Bedford, New York. Needless to say, I died. That home became a part of my mental vision board, and I became determined to work my hardest until I could own a home so dreamy that it could fit a garden. Just as Ms. Martha has inspired me in my life and career, she also planted the seed of an East Coast–style white cottage with plenty of room to grow food around. So when I saw this home and learned that it was literally modeled after a home in East Hampton, a rarity on the West Coast, especially in Chula Vista, I figured it was meant to be.

But going back to no money. All you religious folks will appreciate this. The day after I saw the home was the first Friday of the month, and every first Friday they held a formal mass at my son's school, which

I tried to attend. Sitting at the church, I quite literally told my mom in heaven and whoever else was listening that I wasn't going to stress, that if it was meant to be, I would find a way to get that house. I swear to you on my mom's soul in heaven, sitting in the back row, my phone buzzed with a text message alerting me of a deposit in my bank account on an endorsement deal payment that had been delayed for months. Mass wasn't over, but I politely excused myself, went outside to call the Realtor, and told him I was ready to make the down payment. And just like that, the house was mine.

I moved in almost immediately, and for six months Fau, Yogo, and I camped out in the guest bedroom, the only furnished bedroom in the home, while they worked on the rest of the house. It took a good year to furnish and finish the first story, and the second story stayed untouched for a year and a half. It was certainly a labor of love.

Four years, two kids (plus a third on the way), a new (and much bigger) dog, a fiancé, an entire staff, and a 1,400-square-foot edible garden later—here we are at Casa Marcela, writing books, developing recipes, filming shows, orchestrating photo shoots, and hosting the most amazing Christmas dinners I could have ever imagined.

Food is our life. For my fiancé, Philip (known as Felipe in this *casa*), and I, it's all we talk about. What will we have for dinner? What's growing in the garden? What wine will he have it with? Will the kids eat it? Should we make extra in case my nieces come? What should I get from the market?

It is our happy place. It is our life. Both of us work to the point of insanity. He, in fact, spends half the week in LA. I spend a lot of my time in New York and traveling to other places. My son Fau spends plenty of time in Tijuana, the Mexican side of the border, with his dad. So when we are all here at the house and prepping a family dinner, we cherish those moments like you have no idea. This is when the roller coaster stops for a few hours. Sometimes I'll go and give the baby a bath, get him ready for bed, and come back an hour later only to find Felipe still sitting at the head of the table nursing that same glass of wine like he just doesn't want it to ever be over.

The only thing I love more than this home is my family living in it.

In this book, I walk you through that whole process, mostly with recipes, but also with the stories and photos of all the craziness and love that exists within these walls. When I dreamt up this book, I knew we weren't going to shoot it in a studio. We were going to shoot it here in my kitchen, in my garden, and with my food, friends, kids, and family. It would be a true depiction and a step-by-step of how a meal or a party comes together at Casa Marcela.

In terms of the food (this is, after all, a cookbook), writing about Mexican cooking can be complicated. In fact, it's very complicated. Mexican cuisine, along with classic French cuisine, was declared Intangible Cultural Heritage of Humanity by UNESCO in 2010. That's a big deal. People in my country are very serious about their *mole*. It also complicates things when you're trying to make a career in cooking, and if you were raised in Mexico, then Mexican food is your specialty. See, I grew up in Tijuana, as I've mentioned seven million times with enormous pride in the course of my career. We're a relatively newer city, with urban settlements

that began in 1889. We, and our food, haven't been around since pre-Hispanic times, as have much of the food and recipes from central Mexico. In fact, our friends in central Mexico have sometimes been mortified at our Baja renditions of traditional Mexican food. We like to have fun over here in Baja. We don't really follow rules. We have access to the most amazing ingredients because of the Pacific Ocean and the Mediterranean-like weather. We haven't worried as much about the history as we've worried about food just tasting really darn good. And that's what I grew up with. Yes, there were also a lot of the traditional dishes in my meals growing up, like *mole*, *pipián*, *chilaquiles*, enchiladas . . . all of them. Yet some of my favorite meals were the ones prepared in restaurants that fused Mexican ingredients with other international cuisines like chipotle California sushi rolls, *pasilla* osso buco, and Mediterranean octopus tostadas. That's what the Tijuana restaurant scene became known for. A very well-known TV chef, who shall remain nameless, was once asked where to find the best food in San Diego, and by food they meant food in general, not just Mexican food, and without hesitation, he said Tijuana. I wholeheartedly agree but must admit, it hasn't been easy sharing my recipes at times. I can't share on TV how we used to make tamales at my house without getting a few angry comments on how *that IS NOT how you make real tamales!*

I was once at a very big food festival on the Yucatán coast of Mexico doing a cooking demo with a chef, who shall also remain nameless, who was verbally attacked by a woman in the audience for sharing a recipe that wasn't authentic. The woman looked absolutely insane yelling at him. She was crying—real tears happening. I believe that from the bottom of her being, she just wanted the world to stop thinking crunchy beef tacos and margaritas were representative of our cuisine. She wanted us, or more specifically, she wanted him, a chef who had won a spot on the international culinary scene, to show the world what we were really made of. But here's the thing. Who is to say who is really made of what? Right or wrong, I cook the way my 100% Mexican mom taught me to cook, and I *still* get pushback sometimes. You get sick of saying, "Listen, I know the cuisine, I understand the cuisine, but this is how I cook the cuisine. It happens to be really good, accessible, and fun."

I mean, you'll certainly find a lot of the traditional dishes in this book, but for the most part you'll find me. What my family likes, what the garden gives me, what I cook when I want to remember my mom growing up in Tijuana. You'll find everything that organically happens in the

California kitchen of a cook who was raised in Tijuana but crossed the international border every day into San Diego for either school or fun.

That's one of the most amazing peculiarities of those of us raised near the border: We celebrate everything. Both Halloween and Day of the Dead get a very big shout-out at the end of October, and *Posadas* with piñatas are mandatory during the holiday season.

There is so much talk of walls and division, which all of us on the border find just as funny as we do sad, because for us it's not Tijuana versus San Diego. It's one region. We come and go. We go have lunch in Tijuana only to come home in time for dinner. My home in Chula Vista is literally fifteen minutes from the international border into Mexico and ten minutes south into Mexico is my dad's house. It's like driving from West Hollywood to Santa Monica, sometimes even less when there's no crazy LA traffic.

We live on and love both sides, appreciate both sides, speak both languages, love both cultures, and combine all the foods. So when I made the decision to live on the U.S. side of the border, I made it knowing that I would have to make a conscious effort to expose my kids not only to the cuisine but to the culture that I grew up in. We not only make huevos rancheros for breakfast at Casa Marcela, but Otomi prints are framed throughout the house and Mexican artifacts exist in every room, so that this family and everyone who comes into this home understands that there is a tremendous amount of pride attached to my Mexican roots.

Casa Marcela just grew into a perfect representation of me. Within these walls are the things I love the most—my family, my food, my garden, my culture, my cuisine—and I am honored and happy to share it all with you in the pages of this book.

Every chance I get, I try to remind the world that we are much more than a stereotype. That we are a good, hard-working people, and that we proudly want to share our recipes and culture with you. That we want to combine those recipes and culture with yours. That we want to pass it down to our children. I truly hope you get that from this book. Now, if you'll excuse me, I hear David, my youngest, in the garden, and I want to get out there with him to grab some chiles and tomatoes for dinner. Felipe is on his way down from LA, and Fau is on his way up from Tijuana. My sister and the girls might come by so I need to make sure there's enough salsa for everybody. Business as usual at Casa Marcela.

CASA
Marcela

Small Bites

Botanas

Well, they're not that small. In fact, most of them could be a full meal. We just like to call them *botanas* so we don't feel bad about eating platefuls of them. I, in fact, always have to control myself during this part of the meal because I tend to overdo it and then not make it to dinner. Even though recently I've become a fan of the cheese platter to forgo any real prep, my friends and family truly appreciate when they walk in the house and there's a big bowl of Octopus Ceviche (page 5) waiting for them in the *sala* (living room).

My dad, who has been the inspiration for so many different things I've done throughout my life, was known in Tijuana for throwing the very best parties with the very best food, whether for a soccer match or a Julio César Chávez boxing match or just a good old Friday night. The door to my house would stay open from noon to sunrise the next day. My dad's friends would come and go. By some miracle the tequila barrel never seemed to run out and neither did the *botanas*. By then my brother was allowed to enjoy a beer with the grownups while my sister and I served as waitresses. Yup, we grew up in one of those households where Dad was of a different era and was sure that a woman's place was making her man some burritos while he was out with his buddies. Luckily my mom whipped him into shape in time for us to be sent out into the world knowing that all that talk was nonsense.

I can't lie, though—I reveled in that whole entertaining process. Even though I wasn't making the food, I wanted to arrange the platters, and I had to be the one to take them out to the guests and explain each dish. There was a lot of machismo in my dad's upbringing, but at the same time, I don't think there was a dad more proud of his daughters than he was. I could be walking out with a platter of chipotle shrimp and his face would light up like I was walking back from the Olympics with a gold medal. Now that I think about it, maybe that's where my love of entertaining truly came from.

My mom was highly antisocial, as was everyone on her side of the family. But still, behind the scenes she made sure everything was perfect. She would buzz around the house making sure wineglasses were spotless, platters weren't chipped, napkins were pressed, and flowers were fresh, and then she would disappear into her bedroom when the guests arrived. They had an agreement; you can have all the friends you want over, but no wives are allowed because, God forbid, she might have to come downstairs and talk to them. She tasted every dish, seasoned every sauce, guided me in the arrangement of every platter, but she'd never walk out and say, "Hi." Now, grown up, I understand relationships a little better. You make them work as best you can, and that's what has worked for them. Felipe and I, on the other hand, both really enjoy not only entertaining but cooking together. In fact, in the prepping of a meal before the guests even get here, when it's him and me cooking and the kids running around and Luis Miguel is on the sound system and Felipe's sipping on tequila and I'm nursing a glass of red wine, those are probably the fondest moments I will have of the early days of our relationship.

So here you go. Get inspired, get in the kitchen, and try to enjoy the process as much as the food. Whether it's for a party or a weeknight dinner, you'll find plenty of recipes here, from the very traditional to the more adventurous.

And thanks, Dad, because you were right; this woman's place is in the kitchen. Only it's the professional kitchen, writing books and hosting Emmy Award–winning shows and developing products and cooking for the president of the United States (twice).

Octopus Ceviche

Ceviche de Pulpo

DEPENDING ON WHERE YOU ARE IN THE WORLD, there are many different ways to "properly" cook octopus. We tried it a few different ways because, I'm not gonna lie, I buy my octopus tacos. When living in Tijuana, I had access to fresh octopus in the downtown Tijuana fish market, and I really enjoyed making that trip with my mom on Mondays. Rinse octopus thoroughly before you start to work with it, and take some good pictures for Instagram when you're dunking it in the water (a method used to ensure less curling). My favorite part is the tough, smaller tips of the tentacles, and I prefer to chop the body into smaller pieces. Both of my kids, even the baby, love octopus. It's incredibly versatile and mellow enough in flavor that it pairs well in a fresh marinade, like here as a ceviche or with a bold salsa in a taco.

SERVES 4 TO 6

1 (1-pound) octopus, cleaned (see Note)

1 cup finely chopped white onion

1 cup cored and finely chopped tomato

½ cup freshly squeezed lime juice

2 tablespoons chopped fresh cilantro

1 jalapeño, stemmed, seeds removed if desired, and finely chopped

Salt and freshly ground black pepper

Corn tostadas, for serving

Avocado slices, for garnish

Bottled hot sauce, for serving

Bring 10 cups of salted water to a boil in a large, heavy pot. Add the octopus and decrease the heat. Simmer until the octopus softens and turns purple on the outside and white on the inside, about 40 minutes. Drain the octopus and run under cold water to stop the cooking process. Let cool enough to handle.

Meanwhile, combine the onion, tomato, lime juice, cilantro, and jalapeño in a large bowl.

Once the octopus has cooled, slice the tentacles into 1-inch pieces and discard the head. Add the sliced octopus to the tomato-onion mixture and season with salt and pepper to taste.

Serve with the tostadas, avocado slices, and bottled hot sauce.

NOTE: The head of the octopus tends to come dirty (squid ink color), so rinse it with water until the head is white and completely clean. Cut the lower part of the tentacles to make all the tentacles even. Some people suggest cooking octopus for about 13 minutes per pound.

TIP: If you dip the octopus tentacles in the hot water three times before submerging, the tentacles will curl up all fancy and restaurant-y as they cook.

"En el mar la vida es
más sabrosa,
en el mar te quiero
mucho mas."

Braised Beef Tongue Tacos in Green Salsa

Tacos de Lengua en Salsa Verde

LENGUA (TONGUE) IS SO TRADITIONAL throughout the streets of Mexico that you can pretty much find it in every taco stand and market. It's a tough piece of meat that requires long hours of cooking, but at the end it is so tender it almost melts in your mouth. Traditionally, it is not prepared in a slow cooker (obviously), but you would be surprised how incredibly popular this machine has become all across Mexico. In the end, I think we all just love the idea of set it and forget it. You can certainly do this on the stovetop in a heavy Dutch oven. Bring the salsa verde and tongue to a boil, then decrease the heat and simmer until very tender.

SERVES 6

1½ pounds tomatillos, husked and rinsed

½ white onion, plus ½ cup minced white onion for serving

2 garlic cloves

1 serrano chile, stemmed and halved lengthwise

2 teaspoons salt, plus more to taste

¼ cup loosely packed fresh cilantro, plus more for serving

Freshly ground black pepper

1 (4-pound) beef tongue, excess fat removed

Corn tortillas, warmed, for serving

Lime wedges, for serving

Bring 8 cups of water to a boil in a heavy medium pot. Add the tomatillos, onion half, garlic, serrano chile, and salt. Cook until the tomatillos are dark green and the onion has softened, about 15 minutes. Using a slotted spoon to drain, transfer the salsa ingredients to a blender. Add the cilantro and process until smooth. Taste and adjust the seasoning with salt and pepper. Set aside.

Rinse the tongue under cold water. Cut it into 5 even pieces and season with salt and pepper. Place in a slow cooker and pour the green salsa over, making sure the tongue pieces are almost covered. Cook on high until the beef is tender, about 4 hours. When cool enough to handle, shred the tongue. It should be so tender that it falls apart.

Serve the tongue with the warm corn tortillas, lime wedges, cilantro, and minced onion.

Grilled Shrimp Burritos
with Chile Peanut Butter

Burritos de Camaron con Crema de Cacahuate y Chile de Árbol

THE CHILE PEANUT BUTTER IS NOT ONLY GREAT as a spread for this burrito but
is also an excellent dip for apples or celery or pretty much any crudité! Peanut-based
sauces have become incredibly popular in the taco stands in Baja, with each taquería
adding its own flair. When spread in this burrito, it adds an earthy, nutty, spicy kick that
pairs so nicely with the shrimp. I do think you need the bright and fresh components,
like the shredded lettuce and the crema, to balance everything out. Chile de árbol is
on the spicier side, but you can certainly use a guajillo for less heat and great flavor.

SERVES 6

1 pound 51/60 (small) shrimp,
peeled, deveined, and tails
removed

1 tablespoon salt

2 teaspoons freshly ground
black pepper

1 tablespoon extra-virgin olive oil,
plus more for grilling

6 flour tortillas

1½ cups Chile de Árbol Peanut
Butter (page 140)

2 cups shredded red cabbage,
for serving

⅓ cup sliced radishes, for serving

Mexican crema, for serving

Lime wedges, for serving

Place the shrimp in a glass baking dish and season with the salt and
pepper. Add the olive oil and toss to combine, making sure all sides are
evenly coated.

Heat a grill pan over medium-high heat and brush with olive oil.
Grill the shrimp, turning once, until cooked through, about 3 minutes per
side. Transfer the cooked shrimp to a platter and reserve.

Heat a large skillet over medium heat and warm the tortillas until
pliable, about 1 minute per side.

Place the warm tortillas on a work surface. Add 1 tablespoon of the
Chile de Árbol Peanut Butter and ¼ cup of grilled shrimp in the center
of each tortilla and fold into a burrito. Cut each burrito in half at an
angle and arrange on a platter. Top with the shredded cabbage, sliced
radishes, Mexican crema, and lime wedges. Serve with the remaining
Chile de Árbol Peanut Butter.

Cracklings in Spicy Red Salsa

Chicharrón en Salsa Roja

THEY'RE CALLED "CRACKLINGS," but in this recipe they don't crack. They're not supposed to. It's not like chilaquiles, where you want to preserve some crunch in the tortilla. When you have chicharrón cracklings in any salsa, it will soften with the sauce, and that's how it's traditionally served. This is a filling for tacos or fantastic when topped with a sunny-side-up egg with a side of toast for breakfast.

SERVES 4

2 cups chopped tomatoes

½ white onion

½ cup chicken broth

1 serrano chile, stemmed

2 garlic cloves

Salt and freshly ground black pepper

1 tablespoon vegetable oil

1 (4-ounce) package chicharrón (pork cracklings)

1 teaspoon dried Mexican oregano

1 tablespoon chopped fresh cilantro

Warm corn tortillas, for serving

Put the tomatoes, onion, broth, serrano chile, and garlic in a blender and process until smooth. Season to taste with salt and pepper.

Heat the oil in a large, heavy sauté pan over medium-high heat. Add the salsa and cook, stirring occasionally, until it turns bright red, 9 to 10 minutes.

Add the chicharrón and stir to combine until it is completely coated in the sauce. Remove from the heat immediately. Add the oregano and transfer to a platter. Garnish with the cilantro and serve with the warm corn tortillas.

Grilled Steak and Cheese Tostadas

Vampiros de Carne Asada

THIS IS A DISH FROM NORTHERN MEXICO, where I'm from. In contrast to a regular tostada, where you use beans to anchor the ingredients, here you use melted cheese. Yes, cheese. It's like a steak quesadilla but the tortilla is a crispy tostada. Any salsa will pair nicely with this. I'd go for something spicy.

SERVES 6

1½ pounds skirt steak

2 tablespoons extra-virgin olive oil, plus more for grilling

1 tablespoon salt

1 tablespoon freshly ground black pepper

Juice of 1 orange

1 tablespoon chopped fresh thyme leaves

1 teaspoon dried Mexican oregano, crumbled

6 corn tortillas

1¼ cups shredded Oaxaca cheese or any other white melting cheese

½ cup sliced radishes

¼ cup chopped fresh cilantro

¼ cup finely chopped onion

1 avocado, peeled, pitted, and sliced

Lime wedges, for serving

Place the skirt steak in a glass baking dish. Drizzle with the olive oil and season with the salt and pepper. Add the orange juice, thyme, and oregano and let marinate for 20 minutes.

Heat a grill pan over medium-high heat and brush with oil. Remove the steak from the marinade, letting the excess liquid drip off (discard the marinade), and add to the grill plan. Cook the steak until cooked through, about 3 minutes per side.

Transfer the steak to a cutting board and chop into ½-inch pieces. Keep warm.

Using the same heated grill pan, grill the tortillas, turning constantly, until crisp, about 6 minutes. Divide the cheese equally among the tortillas. Grill just until the cheese is melted and remove from the grill pan.

Top each *vampiro* with ¼ cup of chopped meat and some of the radishes, cilantro, onion, and avocado slices. Squeeze a lime wedge over each and serve immediately.

Spicy Shredded-Chicken and Chorizo Tostadas

Tostadas de Tinga

TINGA, LIKE MEXICAN RED RICE, is one of those dishes where every mother in Mexico has her own recipe, and each thinks hers is the original one. And you know what? You don't argue. You just say, *"Sí, señora,* that's delicious." No matter what the variations are, you always end up with a chipotle-based sauce that bathes shredded chicken and is used for tostadas. The tinga is also wonderful for filling tamales or empanadas. If you're entertaining, make your own tostadas by cutting 2-inch circles out of tortillas and fry them in 350°F oil until crisp. Then build a tostada as directed here.

SERVES 8 TO 10

CHICKEN

1 pound boneless, skinless chicken breast

6 cups water

¼ white onion

2 garlic cloves

1 tablespoon salt

1 tablespoon whole black peppercorns

1 bay leaf

TINGA

4 ounces fresh pork chorizo

2 tablespoons vegetable oil (optional)

1 small white onion, coarsely chopped

1 garlic clove, coarsely chopped

1 pound tomatoes, boiled for 30 seconds, peeled, and seeded

1 cup husked, rinsed, and sliced tomatillos

1 sprig fresh marjoram

1 sprig fresh thyme

½ teaspoon dried Mexican oregano, crumbled

1 (7-ounce) can chipotles in adobo, pureed until smooth

1½ teaspoons salt

1 teaspoon freshly ground black pepper

8 to 10 tostadas, for serving

For the chicken, combine the chicken, water, onion, garlic, salt, pepper-corns, and bay leaf in a large, heavy saucepan. Bring to a boil and decrease the heat to maintain a simmer. Simmer for 20 minutes. Turn off the heat and remove the chicken from the cooking liquid. Reserve the liquid for later use. Shred the chicken.

For the tinga, in a large, heavy sauté pan, cook the chorizo over medium heat, breaking it up, until fully cooked, about 6 minutes. Remove the chorizo and set aside. If the chorizo does not leave 2 tablespoons of fat in the pan, add the vegetable oil. When the oil is hot, add the onion and cook, stirring, until translucent and fragrant, about 3 minutes. Add the garlic and cook, stirring, for 1 minute. Add the tomatoes and cook, stirring, for 1 minute. Add the tomatillos and cook, stirring, for 1 minute. Add the marjoram, thyme, oregano, chorizo, shredded chicken, and 2 tablespoons of the pureed chipotle, reserve the remaining chipotle for another use. Cook, stirring to combine, for another 3 minutes. Add the salt and pepper and stir to combine. Add between ½ and 1 cup of the chicken cooking liquid (broth), depending on the thickness of the sauce. Cook for 5 minutes more to heat through and combine and then remove from the heat.

Place 2 tablespoons of the tinga on each tostada and serve immediately.

"La comida al igual que la vida, cuando son compartidas siempre saben mejor."

Coke-Braised Pork Tacos

Tacos de Carnitas en Coca-Cola

COCA-COLA IN CARNITAS? Yes, both for tenderizing the pork and for that deep, dark, rich caramelization you can only get from cola. This is absolutely great for taco night. Just put the carnitas, still in the Dutch oven, right on the table (use a trivet for Pedro's sake), have all the garnishes and salsas in bowls, and let everybody go at it. Of course, you need to have an actual Coca-Cola to drink with the carnitas!

SERVES 2 TO 4

1½ pounds fatty pork shoulder, cut into 4 pieces

1 tablespoon garlic powder

Salt and freshly ground black pepper

1 cup Coca-Cola

½ cup water

2 dried bay leaves

2 sprigs fresh thyme

1 sprig fresh tarragon

Warmed corn tortillas, for serving

½ cup chopped onion, for serving

½ cup chopped fresh cilantro, for serving

¼ cup thinly sliced radishes, for serving

Lime wedges, for serving

Salsa Verde (page 143), for serving

Season the pork heavily on both sides with the garlic powder, salt, and pepper. Transfer the seasoned pork to a heavy Dutch oven, making sure the pan is small, so the pork fits snugly, which will prevent the meat from drying out when it cooks. Add the Coca-Cola and water. Bring to a boil and decrease the heat to maintain a simmer. Add the bay leaves, thyme, and tarragon. Cover and simmer until the pork is tender, about 1½ hours. The Coca-Cola will caramelize and the liquid will evaporate when finished. Transfer the cooked pork to a cutting board, and using two forks, shred the meat into 2-inch-long pieces.

Serve with the warmed corn tortillas, chopped onion, chopped cilantro, sliced radishes, lime wedges, and salsa.

Lime and Serrano Cured Shrimp

Shrimp Aguachile

THIS, MY FRIENDS, IS HOW YOU CURE A HANGOVER—*aguachile*, which literally translates as "spicy water." You can add water to loosen, but I like a ceviche-like texture. Created in Sinaloa, it is thought to cure hangovers, because with all the spice, you literally sweat out all of the alcohol. The freshest of shrimp is needed, as it is "cooked" by being cured in lime juice. Salt crackers (saltines) are also a surprising but very common accompaniment to many seafood dishes in Mexico. My dad ate them obsessively with pretty much anything.

SERVES 4

1¼ cups freshly squeezed lime juice

1 pound medium shrimp, peeled, deveined, and tails removed

Salt

¼ cup finely chopped red onion

3 tablespoons seeded, deveined, and minced serrano chile

3 tablespoons chopped fresh cilantro

1 cucumber, peeled, seeded, and finely chopped

1 avocado, peeled, pitted, and sliced, for serving

Tostadas or salt crackers, for serving

Pour the lime juice into a medium bowl. Add the shrimp and let them "cook" in the lime juice for 25 minutes. Season to taste with salt and mix well.

Add the onion, serrano chile, cilantro, and cucumber and mix until well combined. Season to taste with salt and refrigerate until cooled, at least 2 hours or overnight.

Serve chilled with the avocado slices and tostadas.

Tacobab al Pastor

THE ONLY THING BETTER THAN A TACO is a taco on a stick! The thing about tacos is they get soggy very quickly. Putting the tortilla on the skewer and cooking it makes it a little sturdier, and it holds up better to the cooked pork and the other ingredients. We've made this on the weekends many times and the kids love them. They seem easier to maneuver than tacos (and are less messy!). Really easy to prep and cook, these are not only delicious but also great for a party platter.

MAKES 12 SKEWERS

1 pound pork tenderloin, cut into ½-inch cubes

1 tablespoon salt

1 teaspoon freshly ground black pepper

2 tablespoons adobo sauce, from canned chipotles in adobo

¼ cup extra-virgin olive oil, plus more for grilling

2 corn tortillas, cut into 1-inch squares

½ red onion, cut into 24 squares

1 cup ½-inch cubed pineapple

Avocado Crema (page 151), for serving

Lime wedges, for serving

12 wooden skewers, soaked in water to prevent burning

Season the pork with the salt and pepper on all sides. Transfer to a medium bowl and add the adobo sauce, making sure the pork is completely coated. Let marinate for 1 hour.

Place the olive oil in a medium bowl and coat each tortilla square lightly. Set aside.

Heat a grill pan over medium-high heat and brush with olive oil.

Meanwhile, thread the skewers, alternating 4 pieces of pork, 2 pieces of onion, 2 tortilla squares, and 2 pieces of pineapple per skewer. Grill the skewers in the grill pan until the pork is cooked through and the skewers are lightly charred on all sides, about 5 minutes per side.

Serve with the Avocado Crema and lime wedges.

Crispy Potato and Poblano Tacos

Tacos Dorados de Papa y Poblano

THESE ARE FANTASTIC AND A TRUE REPRESENTATION of Mexican home cooking. Carb-on-carb perfection that fills your tummy and your soul, this poblano mashed potato can be served as a side dish.

**SERVES 6 TO 8;
MAKES 12 TO 16 TACOS**

1 pound Yukon Gold potatoes, quartered

1 teaspoon salt, plus more to taste

1 cup heavy cream

3 tablespoons unsalted butter

3 fresh poblano chiles, charred under the broiler, peeled, and cut into ½-inch strips

2 garlic cloves

Freshly ground black pepper

½ cup vegetable oil, for frying

12 to 16 corn tortillas, warmed

Place the potatoes and salt in a large, heavy pot and cover with cold water. Bring to a boil, decrease the heat, and simmer, partially covered, until the potatoes are tender, 15 to 20 minutes.

While the potatoes are boiling, heat the cream and 2 tablespoons of the butter in a small saucepan until the butter is melted and the cream is hot but not boiling. Turn off the heat and let cool slightly. Transfer to a blender and add the charred poblano strips and garlic. Process until smooth. Season to taste with salt and pepper and keep warm.

Drain the potatoes and return them to the pot. Add the poblano cream and mash until smooth. Taste and adjust the seasonings.

Heat the oil and remaining 1 tablespoon butter in a medium skillet over medium-high heat. Spread 2 tablespoons of the potato-poblano mixture over half of each tortilla and fold over to form a taco. Working in batches, add the tacos to the oil and fry, turning once, until golden brown and crisp, about 3 minutes per side. Serve immediately.

Tomatillo Ceviche Tostaditas

Tostaditas de Ceviche de Tomatillo

TOMATILLO IS USUALLY BOILED OR ROASTED for salsas, but it's fabulously tart and tangy and perfectly balanced with queso fresco and avocado bits in this fishless ceviche. Here it's used in a tostada, but the tomatillo would also be a great topping for a grilled steak or fish fillet. I like spice, so I add serrano, but a jalapeño would also work here.

**SERVES 6
AS AN APPETIZER;
MAKES 18 TOSTADITAS**

9 (6-inch) corn tortillas

8 medium tomatillos, husked, rinsed, and diced into ⅛-inch cubes

1 avocado, peeled, pitted, and diced into ¼-inch cubes

¼ onion, diced into ⅛-inch pieces

1 fresh serrano chile, stemmed and diced into ⅛-inch pieces

3 tablespoons freshly squeezed lime juice

Salt and freshly ground black pepper

¼ cup crumbled queso fresco

Extra-virgin olive oil, for drizzling

Finishing salt

Using a 2-inch round cookie cutter, cut 2 rounds out of each tortilla to make tostaditas. (Don't throw the scraps out! You can use them for chilaquiles.) Heat a grill pan over high heat. Grill the tortilla rounds until they are crispy and no longer pliable, about 4 minutes per side. They will be dark on some edges and in spots (more flavor!). Set aside.

Meanwhile, add the tomatillos, avocado, onion, serrano, and lime juice to a bowl and stir well to combine. Season to taste with salt and pepper. Add the crumbled queso fresco and toss gently.

Top each tostadita with 1 heaping tablespoon of the ceviche. Drizzle with olive oil, sprinkle with finishing salt, and serve immediately.

Picadillo-Stuffed Jalapeño Chiles

Jalapeños Rellenos de Picadillo

STUFFED CHILES ARE A HOUSE FAVORITE. Poblanos are usually the chile used to stuff, because of their larger size and milder heat. But you'd be surprised to find that other chiles, like jalapeños and dried chiles (usually reconstituted with broth or water), are commonly stuffed as well. With jalapeños you will certainly get a much spicier kick than a poblano, but frying them really mellows them out. If you want something even mellower than that, you can purchase whole pickled jalapeños and just seed and stuff those.

SERVES 4 TO 6

CHILES

Vegetable oil, for frying

16 large jalapeño chiles

TOMATO SAUCE

2 tomatoes, cored

¼ white onion

3 garlic cloves

Salt

1 tablespoon vegetable oil

STUFFING

2 tablespoons vegetable oil

1 baby red potato, cut into ⅛-inch cubes

1 carrot, cut into ⅛-inch cubes

¼ white onion, cut into ⅛-inch pieces

2 garlic cloves, finely minced

1 pound ground beef

½ cup dark raisins

Salt and freshly ground black pepper

Pickled Red Onions (page 149), for garnish

Heat 1 tablespoon of the olive oil in large saucepan over medium-high heat. Add the onion and serrano and cook, stirring, until almost translucent, about 4 minutes. Add the zucchini and cook, stirring, until it begins to soften, about 6 minutes. Add the squash blossoms and basil and cook, stirring, until wilted, about 4 minutes longer. Season to taste with salt, pepper, and a pinch of oregano. Remove the filling from the pan and set aside.

Wipe the pan clean. Heat 1 tablespoon of the olive oil over medium heat. Add 1 flour tortilla, half of the zucchini filling, and half of the cheese. Top with a second tortilla and cover the pan to melt the cheese. Uncover and flip when the tortilla is golden on the first side, about 3 minutes. Continue to cook until the second side is also golden, about 3 minutes longer. Transfer to a cutting board. Repeat with the remaining tortillas, cheese, and zucchini filling, adding more oil to the pan as necessary.

Cut each quesadilla like a pizza into 6 slices and transfer to two plates. Top each with half of the arugula. Drizzle each quesadilla with 1 tablespoon of the balsamic vinegar and 1 tablespoon of the olive oil and season with salt and pepper. Serve warm.

"Bonito es comer con hambre, bonito es beber con sed."

Steamed Mussels in Cilantro Cream

Choros en Salsa de Cilantro

MOST OF THE RECIPES IN THIS BOOK ALREADY EXISTED in my repertoire and daily life, but this dish kind of happened as an experiment in the test kitchen. I just wanted a cilantro soup, something nice and light but somewhat filling and with good body. But after tasting it, I felt the richness of the butter called for some shellfish and a nice, crusty baguette for soaking up all the juices, so the mussels were added. Fausto absolutely loves mussels, known as *choros* in my neck of the woods, so we've happily added this to our family faves list. Make sure you buy them fresh. If a mussel is somewhat open, tap it against a counter. If it doesn't close, then it needs to be discarded. Rinse them under cold running water, and then let them sit in cold water for a good 15 minutes so they can filter themselves clean (they literally spit out excess sand). Then rinse again, gently scrub clean, and they are ready to use.

SERVES 4 TO 6

7 tablespoons unsalted butter

3 celery stalks, coarsely chopped

½ cup coarsely chopped white onion

3 garlic cloves, minced

1½ cups low-sodium chicken stock

Salt and freshly ground black pepper

2 cups firmly packed fresh cilantro (from about 1 bunch), plus more for serving

¼ cup heavy cream

½ cup white wine

2 pounds mussels

1 crusty baguette, for serving

Melt the butter in a heavy medium pot over medium-high heat. Add the celery, onion, and garlic and cook, stirring, until the onion is translucent, about 6 minutes. Add the chicken stock and bring to a boil. Season to taste with salt and pepper. Decrease the heat to medium and simmer for 10 minutes. Remove from the heat, stir in the cilantro, and let sit for 5 minutes. Transfer the mixture to a blender and process until smooth. Adjust the seasonings to taste. Strain the cilantro mixture through a fine-mesh strainer into a medium bowl. Add the heavy cream to the bowl and stir to combine. Set aside.

In a heavy medium pot, bring the wine to a boil. Add the mussels, cover, and cook until the mussels begin to open, about 4 minutes. Add the cilantro cream and bring the mixture to a simmer. Turn off the heat. Discard any unopened mussels. Taste and adjust the seasonings with salt and pepper.

Divide among bowls, sprinkle with chopped cilantro, and serve with crusty bread for dipping in the liquid.

"Una casa se convierte
en hogar cuando
en ella habitan las
personas que amas."

Roasted Salmon
and Pesto—Stuffed Anaheim Chiles

INSPIRED BY THE TRADITIONAL TUNA SALAD, this dish is a lighter version. The salad on its own is a great recipe that can be served as an open-faced sandwich for lunch with a crisp white wine.

SERVES 4 TO 8

SALMON

2 pounds skin-on, center-cut salmon fillet

1 tablespoon extra-virgin olive oil

2 teaspoons salt

1 teaspoon freshly ground black pepper

PECAN PESTO

1½ cups firmly packed fresh basil

½ cup pecans

½ cup finely grated Parmesan cheese

1 garlic clove

1½ teaspoons salt, plus more to taste

1 cup extra-virgin olive oil

Freshly ground black pepper

PICKLED ONIONS

⅔ cup olive oil

2 small red onions, thinly sliced

2 garlic cloves

⅔ cup water

⅔ cup distilled white vinegar

2 dried bay leaves

2 teaspoons crumbled dried oregano

8 fresh Anaheim chiles, charred, stemmed, and seeded, left whole for stuffing

Preheat the oven to 400°F. Line a baking sheet with aluminum foil.

For the salmon, place the fillet on the prepared baking sheet and drizzle with the olive oil. Sprinkle with the salt and pepper. Roast for 25 minutes, until cooked and opaque throughout. Let cool slightly.

For the pesto, combine the basil, pecans, Parmesan, garlic, and salt in the bowl of a food processor and pulse until a chunky puree forms. With the machine running, gradually add the olive oil until the mixture is smooth. Taste and adjust the seasoning with salt and pepper. Transfer the pesto to a medium bowl.

Flake the cooled salmon into the pesto and toss very gently.

For the pickled onions, heat the oil in a large saucepan over medium heat. When the oil is hot, add the onions and garlic and cook for 5 minutes, or until the onions are slightly cooked, but still crispy. Add the water and vinegar and bring to a simmer. Add the bay leaves and oregano. Simmer for 8 minutes, or until almost all of the liquid has evaporated.

Stuff the peppers with the pesto-salmon salad and fit snugly into a 9 × 13-inch glass baking dish. Pour the warm pickled onions over the stuffed chiles and allow to cool to room temperature. Cover and chill for 2 hours or overnight. Serve cold.

SMALL BITES

Cod Fritters with Chipotle Tartar Sauce

Buñuelos de Bacalao con Salsa de Chipotle

WHAT'S BETTER THAN COD? Fried salt cod! Some people,
odd people, find the flavor of cod to be a little too strong. Nothing a little frying won't
fix. And the chipotle tartar sauce can be used pretty much anywhere you'd use
mayo. It's great for fish and chips or on a salmon burger.

SERVES 4 TO 6

CHIPOTLE TARTAR SAUCE

½ cup mayonnaise

2 tablespoons chopped dill pickles

1 tablespoon white wine vinegar

1 tablespoon capers, drained

1 teaspoon whole-grain mustard

1 teaspoon chipotle powder

COD FRITTERS

2 large eggs

2 tablespoons extra-virgin olive oil

¾ cup all-purpose flour

1 (6-ounce) bottle beer,
such as a lager

12 ounces Pacific cod

¼ cup finely chopped scallion,
white and pale green parts only

3 garlic cloves, finely chopped

1 fresh jalapeño chile, seeded,
deveined, and finely chopped

3 tablespoons finely chopped
fresh flat-leaf parsley

2 tablespoons chopped pitted
green olives

Salt and freshly ground
black pepper

Vegetable oil, for frying

For the tartar sauce, place all of the ingredients in a food processor and process until smooth. Set aside.

For the cod fritters, beat the eggs and 1 tablespoon of the olive oil in a large bowl. Add the flour and beer and whisk until well combined. Cover the bowl and refrigerate for 2 hours.

Meanwhile, bring 5 cups of water to a boil in a large, heavy pot. When the water is boiling, add the fish and cook until cooked through, about 6 minutes. Remove from the heat and let cool. Cut into small pieces.

Heat the remaining tablespoon of the extra-virgin olive oil in a large, heavy pan over medium-high heat. Add the scallion and garlic and cook, stirring, until fragrant, about 2 minutes. Add the jalapeño and cook, stirring, for 1 minute more. Stir in the parsley and olives and remove from the heat. Combine with the cooled cod and mix well. Season to taste with salt and pepper. Set aside.

Pour enough vegetable oil into a heavy medium saucepan to come halfway up the sides of the pan and heat to 350°F. Mix the cod mixture with the beer batter and form into little bite-size balls. Place the balls in the oil and fry until golden in color, about 3 minutes. Remove from the oil, using a slotted spoon, and transfer to a paper towel to drain excess oil.

Serve with the chipotle tartar sauce.

Pickled Beets

Betabel en Escabeche

MY FAVORITE RESTAURANT IN ALL OF TIJUANA is called Rodeo and is owned by my dear friends the Pavlovich family. Felipe, not my hubby, but my dear friend who runs the restaurant, is always making sure your food is perfect, the service is flawless, and the restaurant is impeccably clean. They serve mostly grilled meats that are, quite frankly, the best I've had on either side of the border. But the venison jerky is superb. I like to order a *parrillada*, a mini grill that sits right on your table, with chicken, flank steak, and tripe. What I crave in the middle of the night, though, are all of the garnishes. Their pickled beets, which inspired this recipe, are served in a simple, vinegary salad. They pickle everything to perfection: potatoes, carrots, liver. When I was younger and in school in Tijuana we would often stop there on our way home from school and Felipe would kindly give us quesadillas for the ride home. Honestly, he makes the very best quesadillas in the world.

SERVES 6 TO 8

5 large beets, tops removed, scrubbed

1 cup extra-virgin olive oil

2 garlic cloves

1 cup pearl onions

½ cup distilled white vinegar

2 dried bay leaves

6 whole black peppercorns

1 sprig fresh oregano

1 pound baby potatoes, peeled, halved, and boiled until fork-tender

Coarse salt and freshly ground black pepper

Put the beets in a large, heavy pot of salted water, bring to a boil, and cook until tender, 1 to 1½ hours. Drain and cool. Slip off the skins and cut into ½-inch pieces.

Heat the oil in a large, heavy pan over medium-high heat. Add the garlic and cook, stirring, until fragrant, about 1 minute. Discard the garlic.

Add the pearl onions and cook, stirring, for 1 minute. Add the vinegar, bay leaves, peppercorns, and oregano and bring the mixture to a boil. Turn off the heat and let cool to room temperature.

Stir together the pickling mixture, the peeled and chopped beets, and the cooked potatoes and season to taste with coarse salt and black pepper. Let marinate in the refrigerator overnight. Serve cold.

Tuna Empanadas

Empanadas de Atún

TUNA EMPANADAS ARE VERY COMMON IN CENTRAL MEXICO, where the dough is made from scratch. Here I simplify with purchased puff pastry. Make sure you let it thaw overnight in the fridge so it's easy to work with and not too soft on the outside while frozen on the inside. It makes for a great lunch item, an afternoon snack, or an appetizer for a party.

MAKES 12 EMPANADAS

2 tablespoons extra-virgin olive oil

1 cup finely diced onion

2 large tomatoes, cored and chopped (about 1½ cups)

¼ cup chopped pitted green olives

4 garlic cloves, finely chopped

1 (12-ounce) can tuna packed in water, drained

½ teaspoon dried oregano

Salt and freshly ground black pepper

1 tablespoon chopped fresh cilantro

1 (17.3-ounce) package frozen puff pastry (2 sheets), thawed

All-purpose flour, for rolling

1 large egg, beaten

Preheat the oven to 350°F. Line a baking sheet with parchment paper.

Heat the olive oil in a large, heavy saucepan over medium heat. Add the onion and cook, stirring, until translucent, about 5 minutes. Add the tomatoes, olives, and garlic and cook, stirring, until fragrant, about 6 minutes. Add the tuna and cook, breaking up the chunks, for about 6 minutes. Add the oregano and season to taste with salt and pepper. Remove from the heat, add the cilantro, and mix well to incorporate. (The filling can be made in advance and kept in the refrigerator until ready to use.)

Roll out each pastry sheet on a floured surface to a 15 × 12-inch rectangle. Cut each rectangle sheet into 6 even rectangles of about 5 × 6 inches. Place 2 heaping tablespoons of the tuna filling in the center of each square and fold one corner over the filling to the opposite corner, forming a triangle. Using a fork, press to seal the edges. Arrange on the prepared baking sheet and brush with the beaten egg. Bake the empanadas until golden brown, about 15 minutes. Serve warm.

Mexican Turkey Club Sandwich

THIS RECIPE IS PERFECT TO MAKE when you are all by yourself feeling hungry but lazy. I do a lot of traveling, and if the hotel has a good club sandwich from room service, I'm coming back. So I wanted to create the perfect club sandwich—something that would make my soul happy after a 12-hour shoot. And here it is: simple, perfect, delicious. This is also a surprising but very common menu item in cafeterias all over Mexico and a staple at hotels.

MAKES 1 SANDWICH

¼ cup mayonnaise

2 tablespoons chopped pickled jalapeños

3 slices white bread, toasted

¼ avocado, sliced (about 3 slices)

4 (½-inch-thick) slices Spicy Turkey Breast (page 111)

4 slices bacon, cooked until crisp

2 leaves of lettuce

2 slices American cheese

Combine the mayonnaise and chopped jalapeños in a small bowl and stir to blend. Spread the mayonnaise mixture evenly over 2 of the toasted bread slices. Spread the avocado on the third piece of bread. Top one of the mayo bread slices with half of the turkey, bacon, lettuce, and cheese. Top with the avocado toast and repeat with the remaining ingredients turkey, bacon, lettuce, and cheese. Top the sandwich with the remaining mayo bread slice. Cut diagonally into quarters, and skewer each quarter with toothpicks, if desired.

Ensenada-Style Fish Tacos

THESE BEER-BATTERED FISH TACOS ARE SERVED with all the accompaniments we would get when we'd drive down to Ensenada to have them. It's the combination of fried fish, tangy crema, vinegary jalapeños, and earthy tortillas that transports me to the magical beaches of the Baja where I grew up. Any white flaky fish will do. Cod is sturdy and stands up well to the frying, but halibut is also a favorite. Cod just happens to be on the cheaper side, so go for that. The truth is that with all those toppings you'll be fine with any good-quality fillet. Here's the thing about fish tacos: they disappear quickly. So you're gonna be on the fryer, your fiancé will be building the tacos, and your son Fausto will be passing them out. Oh wait, that was me last night. You'll love these, I promise.

SERVES 4

2 cups all-purpose flour

1 tablespoon Dijon mustard

2 teaspoons salt, plus more for seasoning

1 teaspoon dried oregano

½ teaspoon freshly ground black pepper, plus more for seasoning

1 cup dark Mexican beer (Dos Equis Ambar)

Vegetable oil, for frying

2 pounds cod, cut into 5-inch strips (about 16 strips)

1 tablespoon distilled white vinegar

1 teaspoon chile oil (purchased or homemade by steeping any dried chile in warm olive oil to desired spiciness)

1 tablespoon extra-virgin olive oil

½ teaspoon crumbled dried oregano

1 cup shredded Brussels sprouts

Corn tortillas, warmed

Pickled jalapeños, for serving

Mexican crema, for serving

Sliced red onion, for serving

Combine 1 cup of the flour, the Dijon mustard, 1 teaspoon of the salt, the oregano, and the pepper in a medium bowl. Gradually add the beer and whisk until combined. Set aside.

Pour enough vegetable oil into a large, heavy skillet to come 1 inch up the sides of the pan and heat to 350°F. Meanwhile, combine the remaining 1 cup flour and the remaining 1 teaspoon salt on a large plate. Season the fish pieces with salt and pepper and coat with the seasoned flour. Dip the fillets into the beer batter, then transfer to the skillet and fry in small batches, making sure not to overcrowd the pan, until golden brown and cooked through, about 5 minutes. Transfer to a paper towel–lined plate to drain the excess oil. Repeat with the remaining fish.

Combine the vinegar, chile oil, olive oil, and oregano in a medium bowl and season to taste with salt and pepper. Add the Brussels sprouts and toss to combine.

To assemble the tacos, place a warm tortilla on each plate. Top with the fried fish, Brussels sprouts, pickled jalapeños, Mexican crema, and red onion slices. Serve immediately.

DAY OF THE DEAD

According to Aztec Mythology, my deceased mom's soul is hanging in a place called Mictlan, and on the 2nd of November every year she comes and visits us, and we celebrate her and her life. That is completely dependent on the success of the altar we build for her, that is. Is it big enough? Colorful enough? Are the smells enticing enough? Is the food good enough? I sure try my hardest every single year on Day of the Dead. That's what's so amazing about the holiday; it focuses on the color and the celebration of life.

As mentioned, I build an altar every year with traditional elements according to ancient beliefs. You have marigolds to entice with their fragrance and color, water to quench their thirst after a long journey from the other side, and a dog statue symbolizing the dog that will guide them on their way back. Saints and the virgin recall the failed attempt of the Catholics to eradicate the pagan holiday, so they caved and joined in on the fun. Sugar skulls in bright, happy colors remind us that today is a day of celebrating not mourning. The same for the makeup on our faces, it's about life and how, in the end, you can choose to make even what may seem like the saddest of occurrences into an absolute celebration. What I like the most about it, obviously, is the food. Even though it is more common to represent some of Mexico's traditional dishes on the altar like *mole* and *pan de muerto*, tradition also calls for the addition of the favorite foods of the person you are honoring. So for my mom there's Chipotle-Pecan Candied Popcorn (page 245), Buñuelos with Lavender Piloncillo Syrup (page 251), Picadillo-Stuffed Jalapeño Chiles (page 21), and whatever else we remember that she loved, switching it up every year. What always makes an appearance, though, is a can of Mountain Dew soda, a Big Hunk candy bar (which is harder to find every year), and Chicles Pal, brand of Mexican gum she kept a stash of next to her bed.

Because of the holiday's proximity to Halloween and because we like to celebrate absolutely every holiday on either side of the border, the altar stays up for a couple of weeks and is a very big part of our Halloween celebration as well. It's a smash up, and we enjoy sharing the altar. I have a gathering on the night of the 31st and tell my guests that their kids can also bring photos of deceased loved ones that we can add and celebrate with the altar. The point is to keep it happy and light, filled with good food and music, and remind even myself that you choose what filter through which you look at life. My mom's passing was one of the hardest things we've been through as a family, but because of celebrations like this, we are able to celebrate her life and the fact of how lucky we were to have her in our lives. The pressure's on though; last year the altar reached about 10 feet and my personal goal is to make it bigger every year!

Salads
and Soups

Ensaladas y Sopas

After almost ten years of doing television in the United States, I recently started a venture that will have me doing Spanish-language television in Mexico for the first time in a very, very long time. Even though I grew up in Mexico, I thought it was really important to do some research on who watches the type of show I wanted to produce, how they shop, and, more important, how they cook. Here is not so much what I found out, but what I was reminded of in my time with my family and my mom's cooking style in Mexico: The women do the shopping, ovens are used for storage (true, we only used ours on Thanksgiving for turkey, which no one celebrates in Mexico but us few Mexican-American families), we like courses, there must always be a soup, and we don't eat salads. For the soups, it can be something as simple as creamed asparagus, but it must be a hot soup and it must be what you start the meal with. Forget about opening with a salad. I mean, you'll find salads in restaurants, and of course some people do make them at home, but they're not really a part of the home cook's repertoire. Now living in San Diego and with access to these gorgeous, fresh ingredients (not only from my garden but from the farmers' markets as well), of course I make salads regularly. It's just that very few are considered traditional Mexican fare. So instead of diving deep into salad history, I decided to enlist the help of my dear friend Karen Contreras of Urban Plantations, the folks who helped set up my perfect garden, and ask her some tips and tricks for growing your own. In case, you know, you're into salads.

MARCELA: What are the most important things you need to have a successful garden?

KAREN: I think there is a direct correlation between giving and receiving with a garden. The more you give, the more you get! Spending time in the garden, puttering around, you just tend to notice things about plant systems, the interaction of nature, and whether a plant looks healthy or not. Being an active part of the garden will give the best results.

MARCELA: What on earth did you add to my soil that everything grows so darn gorgeous?

KAREN: It's not what we add—it's what we don't add! Using organic methods, rather than adding chemical fertilizers, keeps the soil healthy. Soil is full of microorganisms, fungi, and tiny little critters that help plants take up nutrition and keep the bad guys at bay. We are constantly feeding the soil by adding compost, worm castings, kelp, and organic fertilizers when needed.

MARCELA: People constantly ask me about critters and why they don't eat my stuff. Am I just super lucky?

KAREN: In most cases, when your soil is healthy, your plants are healthy. When your plants are healthy, they don't attract insects. During certain times of the year, various insects start to emerge and become part of the garden environment. Sometimes we begin organic pest control before we see insects. Tomato hornworms are the worst! So as soon as we see the sphinx moth hovering around in the evening, we know they are out laying eggs, so we begin a preventative spray of Bt (a bacterium that interrupts the digestive system of the hornworm). Mostly, though, plants are a lot like us. When they experience stress from under- or overwatering, or they are lacking in nutrition, that's when they tend to become infested with insects.

MARCELA: I've been known to forget to turn my irrigation system back on after I turn it off when it rains. How fast does it need to come back on after heavy rain? How important is irrigation on a schedule?

KAREN: Learning how to properly irrigate a garden is the biggest struggle for people, and there is no simple answer. It's hard to say, "Turn the water on for this many hours for these days of the week," because the

needs of plants change throughout the year. If it's hot and windy, you need to water more often. If it rains, you can turn the water off, but you never want the soil to dry out completely. You want the soil to stay evenly moist, like a wrung-out washcloth, so that you keep your soil organisms alive and healthy. If soil dries out completely, it will take forever to rehydrate and for all our friendly soil biology to return. Most homeowners are really busy and they forget to water sometimes. Having an automated system helps keep plants from relying on our imperfections. Automated systems are not the end-all solution for irrigating, however. We still have to keep our eyes on the plants and our hands in the soil so the plants do not become stressed.

MARCELA: What would you suggest people plant if they are beginners?

KAREN: Broccoli is really easy to grow, and it is so incredibly delicious right out of the garden. I think the most important thing for a beginner to do is to grow what is in season. For example, you wouldn't want to try lettuce in the middle of summer—it's too hot! Melons in the winter will struggle, because they need more heat. Peppers, eggplants, and tomatoes are all easy to grow in a summer garden.

MARCELA: When I asked you to create a garden for me, what did you envision?

KAREN: I saw you in your beautiful kitchen with a stack of fresh peppers, tomatoes, cilantro, and onions. In my mind's eye, I saw you run out to your garden to grab a handful of some wonderful herb you had forgotten to pick, dash back into the kitchen, and continue chopping and cooking. And there was a delicious aroma in the air. I saw you with your kids in the garden, baskets overflowing with flowers and veggies, and I saw you entertaining family and friends, sipping wine in the garden as the stars came out. All of these things are what come into my mind when I think of your garden.

MARCELA: What's the easiest way to figure out which plants can share beds?

KAREN: That's a good question! Plants that have the same water requirements do best together. Woody herbs grow well together and fast-growing lettuce and cilantro make good companions in the same beds. Mainly it's water needs and seasonality that make good plant neighbors.

MARCELA: What's special about having a garden in California and our perfect climate?

KAREN: We can grow year-round! We can harvest delicious beets, peas, lettuce, and cabbage in the winter, and spicy peppers, tomatillos, and beautiful chard in the summer. And the best thing, in my opinion, is that we can grow citrus and avocados! Fresh limes, lemons, and oranges—wow! Nothing tastes better than picking an orange off the tree and eating it fresh!

MARCELA: What are the easiest herbs to grow?

KAREN: Parsley, basil, cilantro. I love lemon thyme, bay leaves, and rosemary, and oregano grows like a weed!

MARCELA: What are some tips and tricks for a successful garden?

KAREN: I think being aware is the most important thing in gardening. We humans get so busy in our lives, we forget to smell the roses, to turn over a new leaf, and to play in the dirt. Just something as simple as sitting in the garden, looking at everything, and letting our minds wander will give us an awareness of the plants, the insects, and ourselves. Nurturing our gardens is therapeutic; it can create self-worth and the understanding of how life works. And really, it's not just about eating; it's about feeding our souls and creating a healthy environment to live in.

So there you have it! Thanks, Karen. Now go grow a garden and make yourself a salad.

Prosciutto Salad on a Stick

I'VE BEEN MAKING THIS SALAD FOR A DECADE, and it's always such a huge hit.
It's all the flavors conveniently wrapped up on a stick, no utensils necessary!
They make a great addition to any buffet because they add height and
are really decorative, not to mention absolutely delicious.

MAKES 12
SALAD STICKS

1½ cups baby arugula

1 teaspoon extra-virgin olive oil

½ teaspoon balsamic vinegar

Salt and freshly ground
black pepper

12 slices prosciutto

½ cup honey Dijon mustard

12 grissini (thin bread sticks)

Toss the arugula, olive oil, and balsamic vinegar in a medium bowl until well coated. Season to taste with salt and pepper and toss again.

Lay 1 slice of the prosciutto flat on a cutting board horizontally. Smear with about 1 teaspoon of the mustard (you can use more or less if desired). Line the prosciutto with a few leaves of the dressed arugula. Wrap the prosciutto-arugula slice around the upper portion of a grissini stick at an angle, slightly overlapping. Repeat for the remaining 11 portions.

Serve standing up in a Mason jar with the prosciutto portion on top.

Pomegranate and Chicken Salad Lettuce Cups

THERE ARE A MILLION THINGS YOU CAN DO with a rotisserie chicken from the supermarket, and this has to be one of my favorites because, as simple as this recipe is, it takes chicken to a whole new level of sophistication. Tart pomegranates make the perfect counterpoint to roasted chicken and salty-creamy feta cheese. I like to serve them in butter lettuce cups, but this is a great little lunch salad as well.

SERVES 6

⅓ cup extra-virgin olive oil

¼ cup freshly squeezed lemon juice

1 teaspoon honey

2 cups pomegranate seeds

1½ cups ¼-inch cubes cooked chicken breast

¾ cup crumbled feta cheese

¼ cup chopped fresh mint

Salt and freshly ground black pepper

1 head butter lettuce, separated into leaves, for serving

Whisk the olive oil, lemon juice, and honey together in a small bowl until well combined.

Combine the pomegranate seeds, chicken, feta cheese, and mint in a medium bowl. Pour the dressing over and toss gently to combine. Taste and adjust the seasonings with salt and pepper.

Serve the salad in the lettuce cups.

Cucumber, Kohlrabi, and Spinach Salad

THIS IS ONE OF THOSE THINGS THAT HAPPENS every weekend here at the house. Felipe, my fiancé, lives in Los Angeles, and we have this ritual where he stops and gets one of our favorite wines—Tignanello, Badia di Passignano, or Stags' Leap— grills up some sirloin, and roasts Brussels sprouts (page 130), and I'll pick whatever's fresh from the garden and make a salad. I couldn't even limit this salad to a season because in this perfect Cali weather (don't hate us), all of these ingredients grow pretty much year-round. It's just freshness on a plate. I get that you might not have kohlrabi in the backyard, but I would certainly recommend hitting the farmers' market before the supermarket to try to source the ingredients. Every human being needs to know the difference in flavor between conventionally farmed, inorganic, traveled produce and organically grown, fresh produce. I'm well aware we don't all have access to these kinds of ingredients, or we simply don't have the budget. I get it. Sometimes I purchase my six-pack of romaine hearts from the big-box store. We have to do what we have to do, but when it comes to dishes whose flavors come from fully raw ingredients, focus on the source. The cleaner and fresher, the better. It's really fun when you see it with kids. Do a side-by-side taste test of raw broccoli from the farmers' market and from the supermarket. It's sweet versus pungent. Tender versus tough. Delicious versus just-edible. That's how you make a kid eat his veggies! You buy them fresh.

SERVES 4

4 cups loosely packed spinach

Juice of 1 lemon

4 tablespoons extra-virgin olive oil

Sea salt and freshly ground black pepper

1 tablespoon apple cider vinegar

1 tablespoon coarsely chopped fresh lemon thyme or regular thyme

1 tablespoon coarsely chopped fresh mint

2 bunches red radishes, thinly sliced

1 hothouse cucumber, unpeeled, thinly sliced

1 kohlrabi, thinly sliced

1 shallot, thinly sliced

Place the spinach on a platter and drizzle with half of the lemon juice, 1 tablespoon of the olive oil, and salt and pepper to taste. Set aside.

Whisk the remaining lemon juice, remaining 3 tablespoons olive oil, vinegar, lemon thyme, mint, and salt and pepper to taste in a small bowl until combined. Toss the radishes, cucumber, kohlrabi, and shallots with the lemon dressing and serve over the spinach.

"Ensalada y visita…poquita."

Massaged Kale–Cilantro Salad

KALE IS EVERYWHERE THESE DAYS, and it's not going away anytime soon, which is a good thing because not only is it incredibly good for you, but it's also very easy to grow. I always have a ton of it in my garden. Giving it a good massage makes it tender and better able to absorb the dressing. Gently rub the dressing into the shredded leaves using your (very clean) fingers. As for the dressing, this is a recipe form my aunt Marcela and is incredibly versatile. You can use it to dress any salad, and it's also great as a crema to drizzle on a fish taco or as a dipping sauce for crudités.

SERVES 2

2 cups firmly packed fresh cilantro
(from about 1 bunch)

¼ cup canola oil

¼ cup plain yogurt

1 tablespoon distilled white vinegar

1 garlic clove

Salt and freshly ground
black pepper

4 cups kale, stems removed
and leaves shredded

⅓ cup drained, canned chickpeas

¼ cup crumbled tortilla chips

¼ cup crumbled queso fresco

¼ cup pomegranate seeds

Put the cilantro, canola oil, yogurt, vinegar, and garlic in a blender and process until smooth. Season to taste with salt and pepper.

In a large bowl, combine the shredded kale and the dressing. Using your hands, gently massage the kale and mix until the dressing is evenly incorporated, about 2 minutes. Transfer the dressed kale to a serving platter and garnish with the chickpeas, tortilla strips, queso fresco, and pomegranate seeds. Serve immediately.

Watermelon, Queso Fresco, and Mint Salad

ALL OF A SUDDEN WATERMELON SALADS ARE EVERYWHERE. I grew up eating watermelon sprinkled with salt, so I'm used to the savory profile, but, until recently, had never really had it with cheese and/or greens. It's just an incredibly light and refreshing combo that's great for an outdoor summer party. For a nicer presentation, carefully scoop out the watermelon flesh and use the hollowed-out watermelon as a serving dish. If it's moving around too much because of the round base, just cut a sliver off the bottom to flatten.

SERVES 8 TO 10

8 cups cubed watermelon

1 cup peeled and cubed jicama

¼ cup coarsely chopped fresh cilantro

¼ cup chopped fresh basil (preferably cut into chiffonade)

1 tablespoon freshly grated lime zest

1 tablespoon chopped fresh chives

1 tablespoon sliced scallion, white and pale green parts only

1 jalapeño chile, seeded, deveined, and minced

3 tablespoons extra-virgin olive oil

2 tablespoons freshly squeezed lime juice

1 tablespoon freshly squeezed lemon juice

Salt and freshly ground black pepper

½ cup crumbled queso fresco

1 tablespoon chopped fresh mint

Combine the watermelon and jicama in a large bowl. Add the cilantro, basil, lime zest, chives, scallion, and jalapeño. Mix well to evenly incorporate.

In a small bowl, combine the olive oil, lime juice, and lemon juice and mix well. Season to taste with salt and pepper and drizzle over the watermelon-jicama mixture. Toss in the crumbled queso fresco and mint. Check the seasoning and add more salt and pepper if needed.

Serve in the hollowed-out watermelon halves immediately or cover and chill for up to 2 hours.

Chickpea and Bean Salad

YOU CAN ABSOLUTELY GO THROUGH THE PROCESS of soaking and cooking
both the chickpeas and the beans, but sometimes you just want to mix a few ingredients
in a couple of minutes and get something both healthy and filling. Canned organic
beans and chickpeas are always in my pantry and always end up getting sprinkled
on my quick lunch concoctions. If you can't find cotija cheese, use a mild feta.
You just want that addition of salty, crumbly cheese.

SERVES 2 TO 4

2 (15.5-ounce) cans chickpeas,
drained and rinsed

1 (15.5-ounce) can red kidney
beans, drained and rinsed

1 cup crumbled cotija cheese

2 tablespoons finely chopped
fresh chives

2 tablespoons finely chopped
fresh cilantro

1 tablespoon finely chopped
fresh thyme

1 tablespoon finely chopped
fresh oregano

¼ cup extra-virgin olive oil

¼ tablespoon freshly squeezed
lemon juice

Salt and freshly ground
black pepper

Place the chickpeas, kidney beans, and crumbled cheese in a medium
bowl and set aside.

In a small bowl, combine the fresh herbs, olive oil, and lemon juice
and mix well. Add the herb mixture to the beans and crumbled cheese
and mix until well combined. Season to taste with salt and pepper.

Zucchini, Fennel, and Mint Salad

FRESH, FRESH, AND MORE FRESH RIGHT HERE. Fennel is one of those things that you really want to try to source from the farmers' market. I grow it in my garden but the bulbs are so small that I always have to go out and get some more. I have to admit, it took a while to understand and appreciate the licorice-like flavor of fennel, and to this day, I don't love it cooked. But toss it in a salad with bright, fresh ingredients, and I find it absolutely delicious. One of the first meals I had at Felipe's mom's house was a very simple tossed greens salad with thinly sliced fennel, olive oil, and lemon juice. It was divine. Mrs. Zonia Button also grows her own greens and fennel and was a big inspiration for the creation of my garden.

SERVES 2

2 tablespoons freshly squeezed
lemon juice

2 tablespoons extra-virgin olive oil

1 tablespoon sherry vinegar

Salt and freshly ground
black pepper

2 medium zucchini, sliced into
⅛-inch-thick rounds

1 fennel bulb, sliced into
⅛-inch-thick rounds

¼ red onion, thinly sliced

2 tablespoons chopped fresh mint

Combine the lemon juice, olive oil, and sherry vinegar in a medium bowl and whisk to blend. Season to taste with salt and pepper. Add the zucchini, fennel, onion, and mint and toss to combine. Taste and adjust the seasonings with salt and pepper.

Mexican Ramen

THERE IS A HUGE INFLUENCE OF ASIAN CUISINE in Baja cooking. We have a very large Chinese community in Mexicali, the Baja state capital that's east of Tijuana. There you will find some of the best, most authentic Chinese food in all of Mexico and, some say, on this continent! Recently, though, ramen has become hugely popular. As opposed to the fare you find in those very authentic Chinese restaurants, ramen has been popping up fused with traditional Mexican ingredients. In fact, there's this one food truck in Tijuana that serves just ramen with different seasoning and toppings all inspired by regional Mexican cuisine. Here, it's almost like ramen and pozole got together and had a love child. It's a hearty soup that will be loved by kids and adults alike. Just put out the noodles and let diners add their own toppings.

SERVES 8 TO 10

1 pound oxtails

2 carrots, coarsely chopped

2 celery stalks, coarsely chopped

½ white onion

2 garlic cloves, mashed

2 dried bay leaves

½ tablespoon whole black peppercorns

12 cups water

Salt and freshly ground black pepper

1 (10-ounce) bag egg noodles, cooked according to package directions

2 cups shredded green cabbage, for serving

1 cup loosely packed fresh Thai basil leaves or regular basil, for serving

½ cup fresh cilantro leaves, for serving

3 medium radishes, thinly sliced, for serving

3 fresh chiles de árbol, stemmed and cut into rounds, for serving

Bottled hot sauce, for serving

Soy sauce, for serving

Lime wedges, for serving

Combine the oxtails, carrots, celery, onion, garlic, bay leaves, and peppercorns in a large, heavy pot. Cover with the water and bring to a boil. Decrease the heat to medium-low, cover, and simmer for 1½ hours, skimming the fat as needed (at least twice during the cooking process). Once the oxtails are tender, strain the broth through a fine-mesh sieve. Discard the vegetables and return the oxtails and strained broth to the pot. Season to taste with salt and pepper.

Divide the cooked noodles among the serving bowls. Top with the oxtail and broth and serve with the cabbage, Thai basil, cilantro, radishes, chiles de árbol, hot sauce, soy sauce, and lime wedges.

Bean Cream Soup

Crema de Frijol

I DIDN'T GROW UP EATING SALADS, but I did grow up with a lot of soups. In fact, it was an unspoken rule that the *comida*, our version of dinner and the biggest meal of the day, had to be a multicourse event. There always had to be a soup, a main course (with protein, starch, and veggies), and something sweet at the end. Often we began our meals with this very bean soup. I would top it with a huge dollop of crema or sour cream, plenty of salt, and some very un-Mexican grated Parmesan cheese.

SERVES 4 TO 6

2 cups dried pinto beans, soaked in water overnight and drained

½ white onion

1 fresh serrano chile

1 garlic clove

1 tablespoon fresh cilantro leaves

8 cups water

Salt and freshly ground black pepper

1 cup crumbled queso fresco

1 cup crumbled chicharrón (pork cracklings)

1 avocado, peeled, pitted, and cut into cubes

½ cup corn tortilla strips (from about 2 tortillas)

¼ cup Mexican crema

Fried guajillo rings, from 3 chiles (see Note)

Put the dried beans, onion, serrano chile, garlic, and cilantro in a large, heavy pot and cover with the water. Bring to a boil, decrease the heat, cover, and simmer until the beans are tender, about 1 hour. Season to taste with salt.

Let cool briefly, then transfer the beans with everything from the pot except the chile to a blender and process until smooth.

Return the soup to the pot and bring to a simmer over medium heat. Add water to adjust the consistency as desired. Season to taste with salt and pepper.

Divide the soup among serving bowls and garnish with the queso fresco, chicharrón, avocado, tortilla strips, Mexican crema, and guajillo rings.

NOTE: Fried guajillo rings are a traditional garnish in many Mexican dishes. To prepare, stem fresh guajillo chiles and cut into ⅛-inch rounds. Heat 2 tablespoons of vegetable oil in a skillet over medium-high heat. Fry the chile rounds until crisp, about 1 minute per side. Remove from the heat and transfer to paper towels to drain excess oil.

Red Chile and Short Rib Stew

Mole de Olla

YOU'D THINK THAT BECAUSE THIS IS CALLED A *MOLE*, you'd end up with a thick soup texture, but it's actually the total opposite. It's a very light but intensely flavorful broth to which you add a whole bunch of veggies and short ribs for a soul-satisfying dish that's perfect for the winter months.

SERVES 4

1 pound boneless short ribs

1 white onion, halved, plus ½ cup chopped white onion, for serving

4 garlic cloves

2 dried bay leaves

2 sprigs fresh cilantro

1 tablespoon salt, plus more to taste

6 cups water

3 dried guajillo chiles, stemmed and seeded

3 dried pasilla chiles, stemmed and seeded

3 tomatoes, cored and chopped

2 tomatillos, peeled, rinsed, and halved

2 tablespoons sesame seeds, lightly toasted (see Note)

2 baby red potatoes, cut into quarters

3 ears corn, halved

12 ounces green beans, trimmed and halved

1 large zucchini, cut into 1-inch pieces

¼ cup chopped fresh cilantro leaves, for serving

Lime wedges, for serving

Combine the short ribs, 1 of the onion halves, 2 cloves of the garlic, the bay leaves, cilantro sprigs, and salt in a large, heavy pot. Add the water and bring to a boil over medium-high heat. Skim the fat from the surface and decrease the heat to low. Cover and cook until the meat is tender, about 1 hour.

Meanwhile, place the dried chiles in a small bowl and cover with hot water. Let stand until softened, about 10 minutes. Drain the chiles and transfer to a blender. Add the remaining onion half, remaining 2 cloves of garlic, tomatoes, tomatillos, and sesame seeds and blend until smooth. Season to taste with salt.

Using a slotted spoon, discard the onion, garlic, bay leaves, and cilantro sprigs from the short ribs.

Add the chile puree to the short rib broth in the pot and stir to combine. Bring the soup to a boil, cover, and cook over medium-low heat until the flavors blend and the soup thickens slightly, about 40 minutes.

Raise the heat to medium and add the potatoes and corn. Cook, partially covered, until the potatoes are cooked through, about 20 minutes. Add the green beans and zucchini and cook for 10 minutes longer. Adjust the seasoning to taste.

Ladle the stew into bowls, making sure each has a serving of meat, corn, potato, green beans, and zucchini. Serve with the chopped onion, chopped cilantro, and lime wedges.

NOTE: To toast sesame seeds, heat them in a medium saucepan (no oil necessary) over medium-high heat for about 1 minute per side. Make sure not to burn them because they will get bitter. As soon as they begin to lightly toast, remove from the heat.

Green Hominy and Pork Soup

Pozole Verde

POZOLE MEANS "HOMINY" IN THE NAHUATL LANGUAGE, in case you want
to impress someone someday. It's a simple soup that's been a part of Mexican
celebrations for centuries. That's what I love so much about Mexican food: the same
dishes that were used in rituals hundreds of years ago are now served at fiestas
celebrating quinceañeras! And a lot of the recipes have only varied slightly.
Pozole comes in different colors, depending on the salsa you add to season.
Yes, you season with salsa. Here, I used salsa verde as the seasoning.
For a pozole rojo, you would obviously use a red, dried chile–based sauce.

SERVES 6

2 pounds pork neck bones

1 pound pork shoulder,
cut into 1-inch pieces

½ white onion

2 garlic cloves

2 dried bay leaves

3 quarts cold water

4 tomatillos, husked, rinsed,
and halved

1 fresh Anaheim chile, stemmed

2 fresh jalapeño chiles, stemmed

1 cup loosely packed fresh
cilantro leaves

Salt and freshly ground
black pepper

1 (15-ounce) can white hominy,
rinsed and drained

Lime wedges, for serving

Dried Mexican oregano,
for serving

2 cups shredded green cabbage,
for serving

Combine the pork neck bones, pork shoulder, onion, garlic, bay leaves, and cold water in a large, heavy pot. Bring to a boil over medium-high heat. Decrease the heat and simmer, skimming the fat as needed, until the meat is tender, about 1½ hours.

Meanwhile, place the tomatillos, Anaheim chile, jalapeños, and cilantro in a blender and process until smooth. Season to taste with salt and pepper.

Add the tomatillo mixture to the broth in the pot and cook until the flavors blend, about 40 minutes. Add the hominy and stir to combine. Continue cooking over low heat for another 15 minutes for the flavors to mingle.

Transfer to individual bowls and serve warm with the lime wedges, oregano, and cabbage on the side for guests to add the desired amount of toppings.

Oxtail, Bean, and Chile Stew

Gallinita Pinta

OH MAN, DOES THIS TAKE ME BACK TO MY HAPPY PLACE! Pedro, the man who cooked for us when my mom was too sick to cook, would make this on special occasions, and I could smell it from the sidewalk when I was coming home from school. A *gallinita* is a hen, which is weird because there's no hen in this soup. *Pinta* means "spotted." So even though it's made with oxtail, when the dish is done, it kind of looks like a spotted hen. Sort of. Well, that's what the person who came up with the dish decided, and it's delicious, so there.

SERVES 6

3 pounds beef oxtails

1 white onion, halved, plus ¼ cup chopped white onion, for serving

1 cup dried pinto beans, soaked in water to cover for 8 hours and drained

3 garlic cloves

2 dried bay leaves

3 dried guajillo chiles, stemmed, seeded, and soaked in 1½ cups warm water

1 (25-ounce) can white hominy, rinsed and drained

1 tomato, diced into ½-inch cubes

Salt and freshly ground black pepper

¼ cup chopped fresh cilantro leaves, for serving

Lime wedges, for serving

Crumbled dried Mexican oregano, for garnish

"Gallina vieja,
hace buen caldo."

Place the oxtails, onion, beans, garlic, and bay leaves in a large, heavy pot. Cover with water and bring to a boil. Decrease the heat to a simmer and skim the fat from the surface, making sure the beans remain submerged in the cooking liquid. Cook until the beef is tender and the beans are fully cooked, 1½ to 2 hours. Using a slotted spoon, remove the onion, garlic, and bay leaves from the broth and discard.

Add the soaked guajillo chiles with the soaking liquid to the simmering pot. Let simmer for 10 minutes. Add the hominy and simmer for 10 minutes longer. Add the diced tomato and season heavily to taste with salt and pepper.

Serve hot with the chopped onion, cilantro, lime wedges, and oregano.

A MEXICAN BAPTISM

In my family we have this inherited obsession with themed parties. My mom needed a focal inspiration point for every gathering, birthday party, first communion, and event. For David's baptism I wanted to bring the feeling of the coast of Baja to my home in Chula Vista and created what felt like the seaside town of Ensenada, where I used to go to get fish tacos, right in my backyard. *Equipale* chairs, party favors that included succulents, olive oil, and fig jam from Baja, plates that resemble Talavera (originals are too expensive to rent), the whole family dressed in blues and neutrals reminiscent of the coast, and, of course, a menu of seafood tacos that would transport my guests back to Baja. There were Grilled Shrimp Burritos (page 9), Octopus Ceviche (page 5) tacos, and

some lobster tacos by my dear friend Chef Luisteen Gonzalez that had my guests coming back for third and fourth servings!

Having a theme makes your parties and even small gatherings easier to plan. It narrows down menu options for both food and drink, color schemes, and even wardrobe options. My mom knew what she was doing, and I certainly felt her presence the day of the baptism. It's like she was telling me that the Pacificos needed to sit in a bucket, informally, just like they do at a Baja beach gathering, and David *had* to wear a mini linen *guayabera* like the men wear at formal beach gatherings in all of the coasts across Mexico. I actually hear her almost every day, whispering and guiding my menus and my every move . . .

Entrées

Platillos Fuertes

Ah, the main dish . . . *el platillo fuerte*. You'll find both very traditional and nontraditional dishes in this chapter. What they have in common is that they have my name written all over them. Herbs from the garden, family recipes, dishes I ate while growing up in Tijuana . . . you name it. If I had it for dinner at some point, it's in here.

Nothing is too spicy because (gasp!) I'm not a huge fan of the burnt-palate sensation. I like to really taste my food, but go ahead and substitute a habanero where I call for chiles if you prefer a kick at your dinner table.

If you want to know where I get the inspiration for a lot of these dishes, then grab your passport and cross the border into Tijuana, something that, as a family, we do almost weekly. In Tijuana, and a little farther south down the Baja coast, you can find some of the best food in all of Mexico. Best tacos in the world? Also in Tijuana. We have a great Mediterranean climate and some incredibly adventurous chefs who aren't afraid to create a cuisine that's special to the region (finally!). The foods that have always been available to us in Baja (fresh seafood, olive oil, Mediterranean herbs, Asian ingredients because of the large Chinese population, all of the traditional Mexican ingredients, and many, many more) have been fused together into what some like to call Baja-Med cuisine. I just call it dinner. So pack your bags and head south. A little too far? Well, here are the recipes that will make you feel like you're right at the dinner table in Tijuana.

Pork Shoulder in Morita-Hoisin Sauce

Puerco en Salsa de Ciruela y Chile Morita

THERE'S A HUGE CHINESE INFLUENCE in the cuisine of Tijuana and Baja because of the Chinese population just east of us in Mexicali. In fact, at our dinner table, soy sauce was a staple condiment and often made it onto tacos and into soups. This dish is inspired by a pork and plum dish that I used to have in one of my favorite restaurants in Mexicali. It is a deep, rich, and flavorful dish that's brightened up with freshly squeezed lime juice and cilantro to cut the fat and take it to the next level.

SERVES 4 TO 6

1 tablespoon extra-virgin olive oil

2 cups thinly sliced leeks
(pale green and white parts only)

3 celery stalks, coarsely chopped

1 cup coarsely chopped carrots

4 garlic cloves, mashed

2½ cups chicken broth

½ cup hoisin sauce

3 fresh morita chiles, stemmed
and seeded (or substitute
chipotle chiles, which have a
similar smoky flavor)

1 teaspoon apple cider vinegar

1 tablespoon salt, plus more to taste

1½ teaspoons freshly ground
black pepper, plus more to taste

1 (3-pound) boneless pork
shoulder, excess fat removed,
cut into 3 pieces

Corn tortillas, warmed, for serving

Lime wedges, for serving

Fresh cilantro leaves, for serving

Heat the olive oil in a heavy medium pot over medium-high heat. Add the leeks, celery, and carrots and cook, stirring, until caramelized, 5 to 7 minutes. Add the garlic and cook, stirring, until fragrant, about 2 minutes. Add the chicken broth, hoisin sauce, and morita chiles and bring to a boil. Turn off the heat and let cool completely. Transfer the ingredients to a blender and add the vinegar. Process until smooth, about 2 minutes. Taste and adjust the seasonings with salt and pepper.

Meanwhile, season the pork on both sides with the salt and pepper. Transfer the pork to a slow cooker and pour the morita-plum sauce over it. Cook on high for 5 hours, or until fork-tender. Shred the pork using two forks or your fingers.

Serve with the warm corn tortillas, lime wedges, and cilantro for tacos.

Apple-Mint Lamb Chops

Chaletas de Cordero a las Brasas con Salsa de Manzana Verde y Menta

ANYBODY WHO'S BEEN HANGING WITH ME ON MY SOCIAL MEDIA for the last couple of years knows I kept the New Zealand economy nice and healthy with my obsession with lamb racks. It's all I craved during my pregnancy, and Felipe, my fiancé, kindly obliged. This dish happens so often at the house that people just expect it with a good bottle of wine when they come over for dinner. I suggest a good mix of herbs but, honestly, whatever is available works. As long as you don't add too much of one herb or another (which could overpower the lamb flavor), any combination works.

As for the *molcajete*, Mexico's version of a mortar and pestle made from volcanic rock: it does make a difference if used. You can absolutely use a food processor, but while the processor's blades cut through ingredients, the *molcajete* grinds out oils and aromas for deeper, richer flavors. Try grinding whole peppercorns in a *molcajete* (or mortar and pestle) and the aroma is just intoxicating.

The apple compote I could eat by the spoonful, and while pregnant I probably did a few times. The lamb calls for something sweet, and the brown sugar, apple, and mint combo is the perfect accompaniment for the fatty chops.

SERVES 2

APPLE-MINT SALSA

½ cup packed dark brown sugar

1 tablespoon light corn syrup

½ cup water

1 Granny Smith apple, unpeeled, diced into ¼-inch cubes

¼ cup firmly packed fresh mint leaves

1 tablespoon apple cider vinegar

Salt

LAMB CHOPS

2 tablespoons whole black peppercorns

4 garlic cloves

2 tablespoons chopped fresh thyme

2 tablespoons chopped fresh rosemary

2 tablespoons chopped fresh mint

2 tablespoons chopped fresh sage

2 teaspoons chopped fresh oregano

½ cup plus 2 tablespoons extra-virgin olive oil

Salt

2 racks of lamb (about 2 pounds total), sliced into individual chops (or buy 2 pounds individual lamb chops)

For the apple-mint salsa, put the sugar, corn syrup, and water in a heavy medium pot and bring to a boil. Add the diced apple and cook, stirring occasionally, until thickened, about 10 minutes. Add the mint and vinegar and stir to combine. Season to taste with salt.

For the lamb chops, place the whole peppercorns in a *molcajete* (see headnote) and grind until coarse. Transfer to a small bowl and set aside. Place the garlic cloves in the *molcajete* and grind until it becomes a paste. Combine the garlic with the pepper. Add the herbs to the *molcajete* and mash until coarse. Add the herbs to the pepper and garlic and mix to combine. Add ½ cup of the olive oil to the herb and garlic paste and season to taste with salt.

Place the lamb chops on a work surface and season each side with salt. Rub the herb and garlic paste on both sides of the lamb chops.

Heat the remaining 2 tablespoons olive oil in a grill pan over high heat. Add the chops and sear for about 2 minutes per side for medium doneness.

Transfer the chops to a platter and serve with the apple-mint salsa.

Sweet Potato Enchiladas

Enchiladas de Camote en Salsa de Tres Chiles

POTATO FILLING IN tacos, enchiladas, gorditas, and quesadillas is extremely popular around Mexico. I wanted something different, and because sweet potato is so popular and has great nutritional value, I decided to make some vegetarian enchiladas. The sauce used here is inspired by the bold flavors of mole, and just like in mole, a variety of chiles are used to provide that depth of flavor. Here the sweet potato works perfectly with the spiciness of the salsa.

SERVES 4 TO 6

1 tablespoon salt, plus more to taste

2 pounds sweet potato (about 3 large potatoes), peeled and coarsely chopped

1 tablespoon chopped fresh thyme

1 tablespoon unsalted butter

Freshly ground black pepper

2 tablespoons vegetable oil

12 corn tortillas

1 recipe Morita, Guajillo, and Pasilla Chile Salsa (page 148), warmed

½ cup queso fresco, for serving

¼ cup Mexican crema, for serving

Fresh cilantro leaves, for garnish

Combine 8 cups of water and the salt in a large, heavy pot and bring to a boil. Add the sweet potatoes and cook until tender, about 20 minutes.

Drain the sweet potatoes and put them in a medium bowl. Add the thyme and butter and mash until smooth. Season to taste with salt and pepper.

Heat the oil in a large sauté pan over medium heat. Fry the tortillas lightly, one at a time, until slightly tougher, about 20 seconds per side until golden but still pliable. (They shouldn't be crisp.) As you work, remove the fried tortillas to a work surface. Fill each tortilla with 2 tablespoons of the sweet potato filling and roll them tightly. Transfer the filled tortillas to a platter. Pour the warm salsa over the enchiladas and top with the crumbled queso fresco, crema, and fresh cilantro leaves. Serve immediately.

Red Chile–Lamb Stew

Lamb Birria

BIRRIA, A VERY TRADITIONAL DISH born in the state of Jalisco, was often made in my home growing up. But instead of using the traditional goat, we would use lamb or beef. We'd only have it on special occasions, though, because it does take a while to cook, but you end up with gorgeous, savory lamb chunks in a smoky, spicy sauce that will make for the messiest but most delicious tacos. You certainly need the lime to finish, not just to brighten the dish but also to cut the fat.

SERVES 4 TO 6

1 tablespoon vegetable oil

1 white onion, chopped

1 tomato, cored and chopped

3 garlic cloves

2 tomatillos, husked, rinsed, and halved

4 dried pasilla chiles, stemmed and seeded

4 dried guajillo chiles, stemmed and seeded

1 tablespoon achiote paste

1 teaspoon ground cumin

2 cups low-sodium beef broth

Salt and freshly ground black pepper

1 (4-pound) leg of lamb, excess fat removed, cut into 3 even pieces

Corn tortillas, warmed, for serving

Lime wedges, for serving

½ cup finely chopped onion, for serving

¼ cup chopped fresh cilantro, for serving

Heat the vegetable oil in a large, heavy sauté pan over medium-high heat. Add the onion, tomato, garlic, tomatillos, and chiles and cook, stirring, until fragrant, about 5 minutes. Add the achiote paste and cumin and mix until incorporated. Add the beef broth and stir to combine. Bring the mixture to a boil. Turn off the heat and let cool slightly. Transfer the sauce to a blender and process until smooth. Season to taste with salt and pepper. Set aside.

Season the lamb with salt and pepper. Transfer to a slow cooker and pour the salsa over. Cook on high for 4 hours, or until the lamb is tender. Serve as is or shred the meat slightly.

Serve with warm tortillas, lime wedges, chopped onion, and chopped cilantro.

Ground Pork Patties in Tomatillo Salsa

Tortitas de Cerdo en Salsa Verde

THIS IS A MIX BETWEEN ALBONDIGAS AND TORTITAS, which are super popular and made out of almost anything. Adding the green apple was an inspiration from a dinner at Laja in Valle de Guadalupe, where julienned apples were served on top of a pork patty. Searing them and then cooking them in a spicy green tomatillo salsa makes them nice and tender. Great with *arroz blanco* and some avocado slices!

SERVES 4

1 large egg

1 green apple, peeled, cored, and diced into ¼-inch cubes

2 garlic cloves, minced

1 tablespoon salt, plus more to taste

1 teaspoon finely chopped fresh oregano

1 teaspoon freshly ground black pepper, plus more to taste

1 pound ground pork sirloin

1 pound tomatillos, husked, rinsed, and halved

½ white onion, coarsely chopped

1 fresh serrano chile, stemmed

1 tablespoon fresh cilantro leaves

1 tablespoon vegetable oil

In a medium bowl, whisk together the egg, apple, garlic, salt, oregano, and pepper. Add the pork and, using your hands, mix well. Form the mixture into twelve 3-inch patties. Set them aside. (The patties can be made 1 day ahead.)

Place the tomatillos, onion, serrano, and cilantro in a blender and process until smooth. Season to taste with salt and pepper.

Heat the vegetable oil in a large, heavy pot over medium-high heat. Sear the patties for about 30 seconds per side. Pour the green salsa over the patties and simmer until cooked through and tender, about 15 minutes. Serve.

Whole Fried Fish

Pescado Frito

SIMPLE AND DELICIOUS, this has been my son Fausto's favorite meal since he was a small kid, eyeballs and all. Make sure you're using a large, heavy pan with high sides so you don't get any hot oil spillage when you add the whole fish. It's very important to pat the fish dry before you fry it. Any excess liquid will just bubble up your oil. I have enough cooking scars to show for it, thank you very much.

Let me tell you about lovage. You will love it. I had never had it until it started to grow in my garden. It kind of looks like large parsley leaves with pointy tips. It's almost like celery, but meatier, and is great for seasoning soups, stews, and broths. You can shred the roots and add them to a salad or a slaw. It's sometimes used as a medicinal herb and was even added to love potions. Yup, that's right: he may propose after he eats this fried fish.

SERVES 2

1 (1-pound) whole branzino, cleaned and scaled

2 garlic cloves

3 sprigs fresh lovage or celery leaves

2 sprigs fresh dill

½ lemon, sliced into ¼-inch-thick half-moons

2 tablespoons freshly squeezed lime juice

1 tablespoon salt

1 teaspoon freshly ground

black pepper

½ cup all-purpose flour

Vegetable oil, for frying

2 cups shredded iceberg lettuce, for serving

1 tomato, chopped into ¼-inch cubes

Bottled hot sauce, for serving

Lime wedges, for serving

Corn tortillas, warmed, for serving

Rinse the fish and dry the surface and the cavity thoroughly with paper towels. Score the fish diagonally, leaving 1½ inches in between each slit.

Stuff each side with a garlic clove and half of the lovage, dill, and lemon slices, drizzle with the lime juice, and season with the salt and pepper.

Place the flour on a plate big enough to fit the fish. Dredge the fish carefully on both sides, making sure to shake off any excess flour.

In a 12-inch or larger nonstick skillet, heat ½ inch of vegetable oil over medium-high heat until very hot; a deep-fry thermometer should register 375°F. Carefully add the fish, letting the tails stick out of the pan if necessary. Let the fish cook without moving it until crisp and browned on the bottom, about 5 minutes. Using a large spatula or tongs, carefully turn the fish. Cook until crisp and browned and just done, about 4 minutes longer. Drain on paper towels.

Place the fish on a bed of the shredded lettuce and sliced tomatoes. Serve with the hot sauce, lime wedges, and warmed tortillas for tacos.

"O ayunar
o comer trucha."

Jalapeño Roasted Chicken

I SAY FOUR SERVINGS ON THIS because that's how many we are in my family, and half of those are tiny Mexicans who don't eat that much. Felipe, my fiancé, and I can easily eat this whole thing by ourselves. One of the very best things you can master is how to roast a flavorful and moist chicken, because you will find endless uses for it once you do. For this one, you'd think there's so much heat from the raw jalapeño, but during the roasting it mellows out to smoky perfection. It also serves as a barrier between the flesh of the chicken and the direct heat in the oven, so the breast stays nice and moist. Think of when you put aluminum foil over turkey breast so you don't overcook it while you're waiting for the thighs to reach 160°F; same deal, but you also get a huge kick of flavor. You can use any chile, really, including serranos, habaneros, or even poblanos if you cut them into strips. I seriously doubt there will be any leftovers, but if there are, the shredded meat is great for tostadas or enchiladas. Enjoy with an ice-cold *cerveza* after a long day at work, and you'll be set for the evening.

SERVES 4

1 pound assorted baby potatoes, sliced into 1-inch pieces

6 tablespoons (¾ stick) unsalted butter

Salt and freshly ground black pepper

½ cup thinly sliced fresh jalapeño chiles

1 (5-pound) whole chicken, giblets removed

3 garlic cloves

4 sprigs fresh oregano

¼ cup fresh parsley leaves

1 lime, sliced into ¼-inch-thick rounds

Place the racks in the upper and lower thirds of the oven and preheat the oven to 475°F.

Arrange the potatoes in a heavy cast-iron skillet just large enough to fit them all in a single crowded layer and dot with 2 tablespoons of the butter. Season with salt and pepper and toss to coat. Set aside.

Carefully place the jalapeños under the skin of the chicken. Stuff the chicken cavity with the garlic, oregano, parsley, lime slices, and remaining 4 tablespoons butter. Season the outside of the chicken heavily with salt and pepper. Place the chicken, breast side up, directly on top of the potatoes.

Roast the chicken and potatoes, rotating the pan halfway through the cooking process, until a thermometer inserted into the thickest part of the thigh registers 165°F, about 1 hour and 20 minutes. Let rest for 10 minutes before carving.

Creamed Rajas–Stuffed Chicken Breast

CREAMED *RAJAS* MAKE EVERYTHING TASTE BETTER, end of story. The problem is, you really never know what you're gonna get. Poblanos, depending on the crop, vary in both flavor and heat. Sometimes they're almost as mild as bell peppers and similar in flavor, and other times they can burn your tongue with the intensity of a serrano chile. So you're going to have to taste them. Putting the tip of your tongue directly on the chile will give you a very good idea of the spice level. I can tell just by smelling them, but you'll get there. Cooking them in rich ingredients like crema and cheese really mellows them out, making them a great pairing for chicken and a perfect weeknight meal.

SERVES 6

6 fresh poblano chiles

5 tablespoons vegetable oil

1 medium white onion, thinly sliced

2 ears corn, kernels removed

¼ cup heavy cream

¼ cup Mexican crema or crème fraîche

½ cup shredded Monterey Jack cheese

Salt and freshly ground black pepper

6 boneless, skinless chicken breasts

Char the poblano chiles directly over the gas flame on the stovetop or under the broiler until blackened on all sides. Enclose in a plastic bag and let steam for about 10 minutes. Peel and seed the charred chiles. Cut the chiles into ¼- to ½-inch strips (rajas). Set aside.

Heat 3 tablespoons of the vegetable oil in a large, heavy skillet over medium heat. Add the onion and cook, stirring, until translucent, about 5 minutes. Add the corn and cook, stirring, for an additional 3 minutes. Add the rajas and cook, stirring, until tender, about 5 minutes. Add the heavy cream and Mexican crema and cook until bubbling, about 8 minutes. Add the cheese and stir until melted and smooth. Season with salt and pepper.

Preheat the oven to 450°F.

Split the chicken breasts horizontally, keeping one long side attached, and open each like a book. Pound the breasts until ¼ inch thick. Season both sides with salt and pepper.

Place 1 chicken breast on a work surface, cut side up. Add about ¼ cup of the creamed rajas in the center of the chicken breast, maintaining a ½-inch border. Roll up the chicken lengthwise and tie with kitchen twine. Repeat with the remaining chicken breasts and filling.

Heat the remaining 2 tablespoons oil in a heavy ovenproof skillet. Add the chicken and cook until browned on all sides, 8 to 10 minutes. Transfer the skillet to the oven and bake for 7 to 8 minutes, until an instant-read thermometer inserted into the center of the chicken roulades registers 165°F. (They will be cooked through but still juicy.) Transfer the chicken roulades to plates and let rest for 10 minutes. Cut off and discard the twine. Cut the roulades into ½-inch slices and serve.

Roasted Tomatillo Salmon

AFTER SHRIMP AND TUNA, salmon is the most-consumed fish in the United States, so I had to give you a good salmon recipe. Even though in traditional Mexican cooking we don't do a lot of roasting (ovens are used for storage, turkey once a year, and flan every once in a while), you'll love this recipe for its simplicity and originality. Tomatillos are usually reserved for salsas, but if you can find them fresh and on the smaller side (they're sweeter when smaller, like Brussels sprouts), they are wonderful roasted on their own. Here they provide a tangy counterpoint to the salmon. As for the salmon, nothing is worse than overcooked fish. In fact, slightly undercooked is much better. You'd be surprised at how quickly it gets cooked through. You just need 20 minutes or so and it comes out perfect and flaky.

SERVES 4

1½ pounds small tomatillos, husked, rinsed, and sliced into ½-inch rounds

2 cups thinly sliced red onion

2 tablespoons extra-virgin olive oil

Salt and freshly ground black pepper

1 (2-pound) Atlantic salmon fillet

1 lemon, cut into 6 thin slices

1 tablespoon chopped fresh chives

1 tablespoon chopped fresh cilantro

White Rice with Basil and Corn (page 128), for serving

Preheat the oven to 375°F. Line a baking sheet with parchment paper.

In a bowl, toss the tomatillos and red onion with the olive oil and salt and pepper to taste. Place on the prepared baking sheet and top with the salmon fillet. Season the salmon with salt and pepper and top with the lemon slices, chopped chives, and chopped cilantro. Roast for 20 minutes for rare. Transfer the salmon to a serving platter and return the tomatillo and onion mixture to the oven. Roast until caramelized, about 15 minutes.

Serve the tomatillos alongside the salmon fillet and white rice.

Braised Chicken Thighs

Pollo del Valle

THIS IS OUR GO-TO WEEKNIGHT DINNER when we want something simple but really flavorful. Chicken thighs don't get as much love as chicken breasts, which is crazy considering they have so much more flavor. That's why I'm a dark-meat girl. Teamed up with Mediterranean flavors, a big trend in Baja cooking, this is a simple and delicious meal that pairs nicely with simple white rice and a glass of crisp Chardonnay.

SERVES 4

2 tablespoons extra-virgin olive oil

1½ pounds bone-in skinless chicken thighs

Salt and freshly ground black pepper

1 shallot, thinly sliced

1 (14-ounce) can artichoke hearts, drained and coarsely chopped

¾ cup low-sodium chicken broth

½ cup chopped pitted olives

½ cup dry white wine, such as Chardonnay

2 garlic cloves, chopped

1 tablespoon capers, drained

2 teaspoons chopped fresh parsley

1 teaspoon chopped fresh thyme

1 teaspoon chopped fresh rosemary

Heat the olive oil in a small Dutch oven over medium heat. Season the chicken thighs heavily with salt and pepper and add to the pot. Sear until golden brown, about 3 minutes per side. Remove the thighs from the pot and set aside.

Add the shallots and cook until translucent, about 2 minutes. Add the artichoke hearts, chicken broth, olives, wine, garlic, capers, and herbs and return the chicken thighs to the pot. Bring the mixture to a boil, decrease the heat to low, cover, and cook for 40 minutes, or until the chicken is tender.

Peppercorn-Crusted Flank Steak
with Mustard Cream

ALTHOUGH DIJON MUSTARD IS NOT the most traditional of ingredients,
my mom absolutely loved it. So rather than a meal you would find in a restaurant
in Tijuana, this dish is something that we would perhaps make on a special occasion.
My grandfather, who was an amazing cook, was greatly influenced by French
cuisine and, to many people's surprise, traditional French bistro dishes were
some of my favorites growing up. The love of all things French wasn't specific
to my family, though; Mexico belonged to the French a while back, and even
after the revolution, all things French were considered in the realm of the elite,
and knowledge of the language, the cuisine, and the décor separated the haves from
the have-nots. It's kind snobby, if you ask me, but the French did give us
some great techniques that are now part of some of our most traditional dishes.
And some ingredients, like Dijon, are a staple in many Mexican households.

SERVES 4 TO 6

2 pounds flank steak, cut into
4 to 6 even pieces

2 tablespoons extra-virgin olive oil

Salt

¼ cup whole black peppercorns,
crushed

1 tablespoon unsalted butter

¾ cup white wine

1 cup heavy cream

¼ cup Dijon mustard

2 garlic cloves, finely minced

1 teaspoon Worcestershire sauce

Drizzle the steaks with the olive oil and season heavily with salt on both sides. Press the crushed peppercorns into the meat, making sure it gets completely coated.

Heat a large, heavy saucepan over medium-high heat. Melt the butter, then add the steaks and cook, turning once, for about 12 minutes for medium-rare. Transfer to a cutting board and let stand for 5 minutes.

Meanwhile, decrease the heat to medium and add the white wine, scraping the pan with a wooden spoon. Cook until reduced by one-fourth, about 5 minutes. Add the cream, mustard, garlic, and Worcestershire sauce and cook until slightly thickened, about 5 minutes. Taste and adjust the seasoning with salt. Turn off the heat and pour the sauce into a small serving bowl.

Thinly slice the steaks at an angle across the grain and serve with the mustard cream sauce on the side.

"A mala carne
buena salsa."

Grilled Beef Strips

Asado de Tira

THE CUT OF BEEF FOR THIS RECIPE, also known as "flanken,"
refers to a strip of beef cut across the bone from the chuck end of the short ribs.
The result is a thin strip of meat, 8 to 10 inches in length, lined with ½-inch-thick rib
bones. The thin slices make for fast cooking on the grill. In Tijuana, these are
usually brought to the table on a grill with other cuts of meat and accompanied
by lime wedges, corn tortillas, and avocado slices.

SERVES 4 TO 6

5 pounds Korean-style short ribs

2 tablespoons extra-virgin olive oil

Salt and freshly ground
black pepper

1 tablespoon fresh oregano,
chopped

1 tablespoon freshly squeezed
lime juice

Mint and Cilantro Salsa Verde
(page 153)

Place the meat in a glass baking dish and drizzle with the olive oil.
Season with salt and pepper, then add the oregano and lime juice. Cover
with plastic wrap and marinate in the refrigerator for 3 hours or up to
overnight.

Preheat a grill pan over high heat and grill the ribs until lightly
charred on the outside, about 5 minutes per side for medium-rare. Let
stand for 5 minutes. Transfer to platter and serve with Mint and Cilantro
Salsa Verde.

Creamy Beer Shrimp–Stuffed Poblano Chiles

THIS IS A SHOWSTOPPER RIGHT HERE. If you are lucky enough to travel
through Mexico, you'll find that there are countless versions of stuffed peppers:
with cheese, with meat, with beans, with dried fruit, and here with seafood.
This simple, rich, creamy perfection fills the optimal pepper for stuffing: the poblano.
Be careful, though, because depending on the crop, they can range from totally mild
to pretty darn spicy. Don't be afraid to smell them at the market: if it stings your nose
a little, you're probably gonna get some fire from the pepper. If spice is what you
are looking for, you can certainly use a jalapeño. They are smaller, so you'll have to
purchase a few more to use up all the stuffing, but they also come out great.

SERVES 4 TO 6

4 to 6 fresh poblano chiles

1 tablespoon unsalted butter

3 garlic cloves, chopped

3 dried chiles de árbol

2 pounds medium shrimp, peeled,
deveined, tails removed,
and quartered

Salt

½ cup dark lager beer

½ cup heavy cream

1 cup shredded Oaxaca cheese,
or any other white melting cheese

Turn a gas burner to high. Char the poblano chiles directly on the burner,
turning with tongs, until blackened all over. (Alternatively, roast in the
oven under the broiler.) Place the chiles in a plastic bag and let steam for
10 minutes.

Gently rub the chiles with paper towels to remove as much skin as
possible. Using a paring knife, make a slit across the top of a chile just
below the stem, leaving the stem intact. Starting from the middle of the
slit, slice lengthwise down to the tip of the pepper (cut through only
one layer). Open the chile like a book and pull out the seeds and inner
membranes. You may need to use a paring knife to loosen the top of the
seedpod. Repeat with the remaining chiles.

Melt the butter in a large, heavy saucepan over medium heat. Add
the garlic and chiles de árbol and cook, stirring, until fragrant, about
2 minutes. Add the shrimp and cook, stirring, until lightly pink, about
1 minute. Season with salt to taste. Stir in the beer and cook until lightly
evaporated, about 3 minutes. Stir in the cream and bring the mixture to
a simmer. Remove the shrimp from the sauce and cook the sauce until
thickened, about 6 minutes more. Return the shrimp to the pan and add
½ cup of the cheese, stirring until the cheese is completely melted. Turn
off the heat.

Preheat the broiler to high.

Fill each chile with about ¼ cup of the creamy shrimp and transfer to
a large glass baking dish. Divide the remaining ½ cup cheese among the
chiles and broil until the cheese is melted and golden brown, about
6 minutes.

Crown Pork Roast with Chorizo and Apple Stuffing

ONE OF MY FAVORITE THINGS ABOUT DOING THE SHOW *The Kitchen* on the Food Network is what I learn from my cohosts. I didn't grow up with too many roasts, and when we did have one for dinner or a celebration, it was rarely pork. On the show, Geoffrey Zakarian made the most amazing crown pork roast with a mustard sauce, and as usual, I wanted to tweak it with the flavors of my childhood. A crown pork roast might not be available daily at the supermarket, so make sure to call ahead and order it if needed.

SERVES 6 TO 8

RUB

2 tablespoons chopped
fresh rosemary

2 tablespoons finely minced garlic

2 tablespoons Dijon mustard

2 tablespoons extra-virgin olive oil

ROAST

1 (4-pound) bone-in crown
pork roast

Salt and freshly ground
black pepper

CHORIZO AND APPLE STUFFING

3 bolillo rolls, or any other bread,
cut into 1-inch cubes

8 tablespoons (1 stick)
unsalted butter

1 cup medium-diced white onion

2 Granny Smith apples, peeled,
cored, and cut into large dice

2 tablespoons chopped
fresh cilantro

1 tablespoons salt

1 teaspoon freshly ground
black pepper

9 ounces fresh pork chorizo,
casing removed

1 cup chicken broth

Preheat the oven to 350°F. Line a baking sheet with parchment paper.

For the rub, combine the rosemary, garlic, mustard, and olive oil in a small bowl and whisk until well blended.

For the roast, season the pork heavily on all sides with salt and pepper and rub the rosemary-garlic mixture all over. Place in a glass baking dish, cover with plastic wrap, and marinate for about 2 hours in the refrigerator.

Meanwhile, for the chorizo and apple stuffing, place the bread cubes in a single layer on the prepared baking sheet and toast for 7 minutes. Transfer the toasted bread cubes to a very large bowl and set aside. Increase the oven temperature to 375°F.

Melt the butter in a large, heavy sauté pan over medium heat. Add the onion, apples, and cilantro and season with the salt and pepper. Cook, stirring, until the vegetables are softened, about 10 minutes. Add to the bread cubes.

In the same sauté pan, cook the chorizo over medium heat, breaking it up with a fork while cooking, until browned and cooked through, about 10 minutes. Transfer the chorizo to paper towels to drain excess fat and add to the bread cubes and vegetables. Add the broth and toss until moistened.

Stuff the chorizo and apple stuffing into the center of the roast until the filling comes to the point of the meat meeting the bone. Transfer the pork to a roasting pan. Roast until the center of the pork registers 150°F on an instant-read thermometer, about 2 hours.

Spoon the stuffing into a bowl. Tent the roast with aluminum foil and let rest for 15 minutes. Slice the meat and serve with the stuffing.

"Estoy más atado
que un chorizo."

Spicy Turkey Breast

THIS RECIPE CAN BE USED in so many different ways. You can slice it and serve it with mashed potatoes for a weeknight dinner, use it in a club sandwich (page 38) for a great lunch, shred it and make *sopes* or *taquitos dorados*, or use it to make turkey noodle soup.

SERVES 4

1 tablespoon freshly ground black pepper

1 teaspoon ground chile de árbol or red pepper flakes

1 teaspoon garlic powder

½ teaspoon chipotle powder

1 (3-pound) bone-in, skin-on turkey breast

1 tablespoon salt

Preheat the oven to 350°F. Set a rack on top of a baking sheet.

Combine the pepper, chile de árbol, garlic powder, and chipotle powder in a small bowl until well blended. Rub all over the outside of the turkey breast and then season with the salt.

Arrange the turkey breast, skin side up, on the prepared baking sheet. Roast for about 1½ hours, until the skin is crisp and golden brown and an instant-read thermometer inserted into the thickest part of the breast registers 150°F.

Transfer the turkey breast to a platter and let rest for 10 minutes before carving.

Pounded Fillet Topped with Salsa Ranchera

Sábana Ranchera

THIS WAS MY GO-TO MEAL WHEN I WOULD VISIT MY DAD at his second home, the Campestre Tijuana Country Club. A *sábana* is a bedsheet, which is meant to describe how thin the meat needs to be pounded for this dish—like a Milanese but even thinner if you can without piercing the meat. I went the traditional route and just topped it with warm salsa, but you can certainly add some shredded Oaxaca or Monterey Jack cheese and quickly broil it, for a salsa-and-cheese-topped fillet. Serve with a good portion of guacamole, refried beans, and warm flour tortillas.

SERVES 4

4 (6-ounce) beef tenderloin fillets, pounded to about 1/8 inch thick

Salt and freshly ground black pepper

2 tablespoons extra-virgin olive oil

1 cup chopped white onion

3 large tomatoes, cored and chopped

3 garlic cloves, chopped

1 large jalapeño chile, chopped

1/2 cup water

2½ tablespoons chopped fresh cilantro

Season the beef tenderloins heavily with salt and pepper on both sides.

Heat 1 tablespoon of the olive oil in a large, heavy saucepan over medium heat. Add the beef fillets and cook until cooked through, about 1 minute per side.

Place the cooked fillets on a plate and cover with aluminum foil to keep warm while cooking the salsa.

Add the remaining 1 tablespoon olive oil to the saucepan. Add the onion and cook, stirring, until fragrant, about 3 minutes. Add the tomatoes, garlic, and jalapeño and cook, stirring, for 5 minutes more. Add the water and bring the mixture to a simmer. Season to taste with salt and pepper. Turn off the heat and add the cilantro, mixing well. Transfer to a food processor and pulse about eight times, or until chunky. Serve on top of the cooked fillets.

"Tener la sartén
por el mango."

Prime Rib Roast

THIS IS A FAMILY FAVORITE that I've made on many occasions.
From TV appearances to Christmas family dinners, it always impresses guests.
All credit has to go to one of my biggest inspirations in the cooking world,
my aunt Marcela. This is her recipe.

A prime rib can look monstrous to the novice cook, but it's actually
a piece of cake to make if you just have a good thermometer and know to insert
it right in the center of the roast to get the proper temperature read. Be sure to
let the cooked roast rest for 20 minutes; otherwise, you'll cut into it and lose
all the juices. If you have kids at the table, which I often do, you can take
a few of the rare slices and pan-sear them in a little olive oil, as kids don't love
the texture of rare meat. And if you have any leftovers, sear the slices
and then chop them, and make yourself the most amazing taco.

SERVES 8

ROAST

4-rib (9- to 10-pound)
prime rib roast (often called
standing rib roast)

Salt

¼ cup Dijon mustard

¼ cup mixed assorted
ground peppercorns

2 tablespoons all-purpose flour

2 tablespoons soy sauce

2 tablespoons
Worcestershire sauce

2 tablespoon ground rosemary

1 tablespoon ground chile de árbol
or red pepper flakes

4 garlic cloves, smashed

About 4 cups low-sodium beef
broth, or as needed

GRAVY

2 tablespoons extra-virgin olive oil

2 garlic cloves, minced

1 small shallot, minced

1 pound mushrooms,
stemmed and sliced

1 tablespoon soy sauce

1 tablespoon Worcestershire sauce

2 tablespoons all-purpose flour

1 cup red wine

1 cup beef broth

Salt and freshly ground
black pepper

Preheat the oven to 400°F.

For the roast, let the meat stand for 1 hour at room temperature. Season heavily with salt.

In a medium bowl, combine the mustard, peppercorns, flour, soy sauce, Worcestershire, ground rosemary, chile, and garlic and mix to form a paste. Rub all over the roast.

Place the roast on a roasting rack set in a roasting pan and add 2 cups of the beef broth to the bottom of the roasting pan. Roast for about 30 minutes, until it is perfectly browned. Remove from the oven and decrease the oven temperature to 350°F. Tent the roast with aluminum foil, making sure the foil does not touch the roast. Return it to the oven and roast for 1½ to 2 hours, until an instant-read thermometer registers 110°F, adding more of the broth to the pan as needed if the liquid begins to evaporate.

Remove from the oven and let rest, uncovered, for at least 20 minutes before carving. Pour the pan drippings into a separate bowl and reserve for the gravy.

For the gravy, heat the olive oil in a heavy medium saucepan over medium heat. Add the garlic and shallot and cook, stirring, for 3 minutes, or until fragrant. Add the sliced mushrooms and cook, stirring frequently, until the mushrooms soften and give up their juices, about 6 minutes. Add the soy sauce and Worcestershire sauce and mix well. Add the flour and cook, stirring to dissolve the flour, for about 3 minutes. Add the red wine and cook until reduced by one-fourth, about 10 minutes. Add the beef broth and season to taste with salt and pepper. Add the pan drippings to the gravy and bring to a boil. Decrease the heat and simmer until the mixture is thick enough to coat the back of a spoon, about 8 minutes.

Serve the gravy with the prime rib roast.

"Vale mas morir de lleno que de vacío."

Kale-Potato Enchiladas Verdes

VEGGIE ENCHILADA HEAVEN . . . Here's what's important in this recipe:
dip the tortillas in hot oil before dipping them in the salsa verde. This will
ensure that they hold their shape. There is nothing worse than a soggy enchilada,
and that quick fry creates a protective barrier so that the tortilla doesn't fully
absorb the salsa. It can get messy. You are, after all, filling a salsa-drenched
tortilla with filling, but it's so worth it. I like to keep a bowl of water and a dishtowel
nearby so I can clean my fingers during the process. Kale and potatoes might
not be what you think about in terms of enchilada fillings, but vegetarian fillings
are often used for this very traditional dish. I added kale because that's what
I always have fresh in the garden, but chard works, or even spinach.

SERVES 6

SALSA VERDE

2 pounds tomatillos,
husked and rinsed

1 large jalapeño chile,
seeded if desired

¼ large white onion

1 large bunch fresh cilantro,
thick stems removed

2 garlic cloves

1 teaspoon salt

ENCHILADAS

1 tablespoon extra-virgin olive oil

¼ large white onion, chopped

2 garlic cloves, minced

2 cups loosely packed chopped
fresh kale, thick stems removed

½ cup Mexican crema

1 tablespoon unsalted butter

2 pounds russet potatoes, peeled,
cut into ½-inch pieces, and boiled
in salted water until fork-tender

1¼ cups shredded Monterey Jack
cheese

Salt and freshly ground
black pepper

Vegetable oil, for dipping

12 corn tortillas

Preheat the oven to 350°F. Have ready a 13 x 9-inch glass baking dish.

For the salsa verde, bring a large pot of salted water to a boil over medium-high heat. Add the tomatillos, jalapeño, onion, cilantro, and garlic and return to a boil. Boil until the tomatillos are olive-green, about 10 minutes. Strain, reserving 1 cup of the cooking liquid. Transfer to a blender with the reserved liquid and blend until smooth. Return to the same (empty) pan and boil until darker green and thickened, 20 to 25 minutes longer. Stir in the salt and set aside.

For the enchiladas, heat the olive oil in a large, heavy sauté pan. Add the onion and garlic and cook, stirring, until golden, about 5 minutes. Add the kale and cook, stirring occasionally, until wilted, about 5 more minutes. Add ¼ cup of the crema and the butter and mix until melted and smooth. Gently mix in the potatoes and 1 cup of the cheese. Season to taste with salt and pepper. Set the filling aside.

Make an assembly line close to the stovetop. Place half of the salsa verde in a cake pan. Add enough vegetable oil to a skillet to come 1 inch up the sides and heat to 350°F. Dip the tortillas in the oil and cook until golden but still pliable, about 20 seconds. Using tongs, transfer to the cake pan with the salsa verde and turn to coat. Place the dipped tortilla on a cutting board and add a scant ¼ cup of the potato-kale filling. Roll the tortilla into an enchilada. Transfer to the baking dish. Repeat with the remaining tortillas, the salsa verde in the cake pan, and the filling. Top with the remaining half of the salsa verde, the remaining ¼ cup crema, and the remaining ¼ cup cheese. Bake until darkened in spots, about 30 minutes. Serve slightly cooled.

SALT

My father had the horrible habit of covering his entire meal with salt before even tasting it, and it would drive my mother nuts. Needless to say, like many of our parents' habits, I inherited that love for everything salty. In fact I have very few cravings for anything sweet and look more for the sweet-salty-sour combinations in Mexican candy like salted plums and chile-covered tamarind. It wasn't until I became a professional cook and was introduced to kosher salt that I realized how horrible the actual taste of iodized table salt was to my palate. I don't even have any here at home. I use kosher salt for all of my cooking and put out all of my seasoned salts, from all over the world, on the table at every meal and let my guests pick their own flavor. There are a few companies in Mexico that have the most amazing of flavor combinations like habanero, orange, ginger, and ground grasshoppers (yup, they do that) from Compañia de Sales. The folks at Mezcal Marca Negra make a *sal de gusano* (ground, dried worm salt; yup, also a thing) that is great for rimming beer glasses and sprinkling on orange wedges when sipping tequila. I fell in love with Mallorca's *flor de sal d'es trenc* sea salt and used their black olive sea salt to top pasta for almost a year, but they have a ton of flavors to choose from. It's worth experimenting with them. I always have pink Himalayan sea salt that I use to sprinkle on the kids' meals because of the beneficial minerals it contains, and even though I find it to be saltier than other salts (if that makes any sense), I really enjoy a light sprinkling of French gray sea salt on fruit. The point is, once you start tasting and experimenting, you'll find that regular table salt has this chemically after-taste that after you identify, you just can't go back. Just thinking of the amount of salt my dad used to pour on his food makes me cringe a little, but at the same time, it makes me grateful because it initiated my obsession with salt.

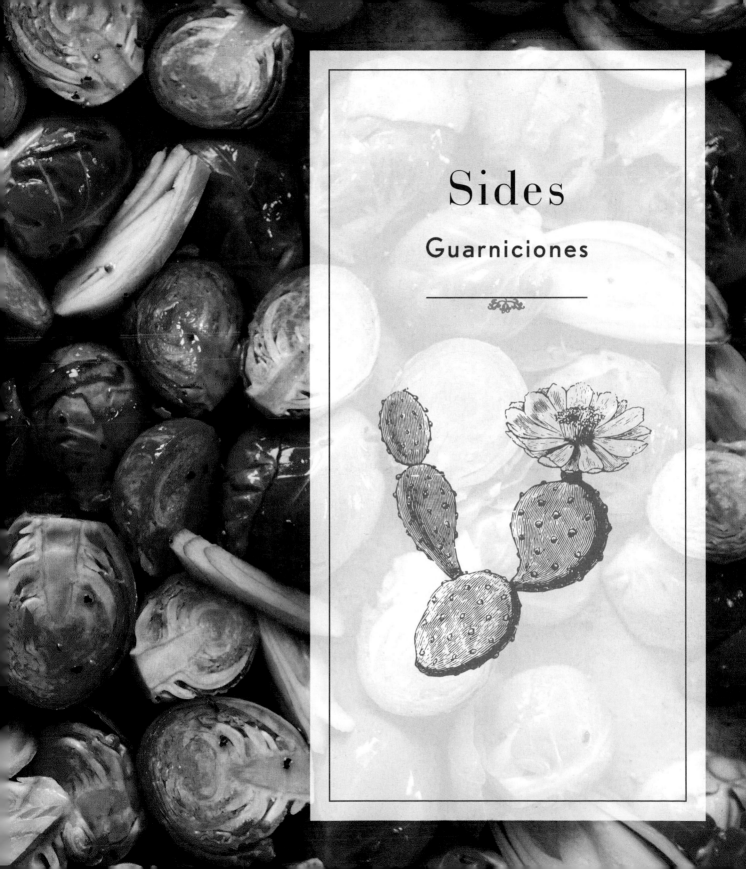

Sides

Guarniciones

It is not uncommon for me to read through a restaurant menu and decide to only order a bunch of sides/vegetables and forgo the entrée. The adults and kids in my family are both very picky about big pieces of protein and lovers of vegetables. So often at the restaurant we'll be all about Brussels sprouts and Broccolini and sautéed corn. I'm blessed and cursed when it comes to vegetables because of the garden. Life is never the same after you eat a home-grown tomatillo.

The secret, my friends, is when you get your vegetables, to look as hard as you can for seasonal and organic ones. Try to hit the farmers' market, ask for what's in season, look for clean veggies. Good, clean veggies are not only good for your body, but because of their superior flavors, are more palatable to the picky eaters in your life. I swear broccoli is sweet when it's freshly pulled out of the ground. Now, I don't want to be the annoying nut telling you that if you didn't grow it you can't eat it, but it's certainly worth the effort, at least for educational purposes and especially if you have kids. We are experiencing the worst statistics ever in obesity and diabetes in both children and adults, so the time is now to try to get super creative in how you serve your veggies. Folks often ask me why it is that my kids aren't picky eaters. Well, they are picky eaters, I just make sure to find the few things that they will eat. The healthy things. And give them zero access (at home) to junk. Out on the street they can have whatever they want but at home I make sure to always stay stocked with healthy veggies I know they like. As for the adults, these sides might be your solution, if not for the kids. The goal is to put dishes on the table that the whole family will eat, and I'm sure most of these fit that description. If you still think you need more options, here's a tip from my ex-boss and former food editor of *Bon Appétit* magazine, Kristine Kidd. Take any given vegetable and put it through every cooking method to see which one you and your family will like the most. That's how you get to know a vegetable. Develop natural sweetness by roasting, kill bitterness by steaming, add moisture by braising, flavor with char by broiling . . . you get the idea. The point is to play and get creative with your food. Invest the time and money in the one thing that makes the most difference in your body and health. These recipes are a good place to start!

Roasted-Cauliflower Steaks
with Pickled-Jalapeño Vinaigrette

I READ RECENTLY THAT THERE'S A SHORTAGE of cauliflower because
it's become so popular on the U.S. food scene. I don't know what took everybody
so long. Roasted, it has a nutty-sweet flavor that is a perfect side for pretty much
any meal, and when it's coming straight from the garden and is the perfect purple color
of that weird dinosaur that has recently made it back into our lives because of
the baby (and thanks to Netflix), it's phenomenal. It's also a favorite among carb
watchers because it's a great substitute for rice and potatoes. I've even made a
pizza crust out of it, and you don't miss a thing. Sometimes I'll just roast the whole
head on a Monday and snack on it during the first few days of the week.

SERVES 4

1 (1½-pound) head cauliflower

5 tablespoons extra-virgin olive oil

Salt and freshly ground
black pepper

2 tablespoons jalapeño pickling
juice, from 1 (12-ounce) can
pickled jalapeños

1 tablespoon sherry vinegar

2 pickled jalapeño chiles, sliced
into ⅛-inch rings, for serving

3 tablespoons shaved Parmesan
cheese, for serving

2 tablespoons roasted and salted
pumpkin seeds (see Note),
for serving

Preheat the oven to 375°F. Line a baking sheet with parchment paper.

Using a sharp knife and starting at the top center of the cauliflower head, cut 1-inch-thick slices, making sure to cut through the stem end. (You may have some remaining florets, which you can roast on the side.) Set the cauliflower steaks on the prepared baking sheet. Brush with 2 tablespoons of the olive oil and sprinkle with salt and pepper. Roast the cauliflower steaks without flipping them until golden brown and cooked through, about 40 minutes.

Meanwhile, add the jalapeño pickling juice, sherry vinegar, and remaining 3 tablespoons olive oil to a medium bowl and whisk until well combined. Season to taste with salt and pepper.

Place the roasted cauliflower on a platter and drizzle with the jalapeño vinaigrette. Garnish with the sliced jalapeños, shaved Parmesan, and pumpkin seeds.

NOTE: Purchase pumpkin seeds that are roasted and salted.

Felipe's Brussels Sprouts

I REALLY LOVE THIS GUY, and I've got the posts on Instagram to prove it. I think the true love started when he made these for me the first time. They are so simple, easy, and delicious, and on our dinner table at least three or four times a week. We are Brussels sprouts obsessed in this house. Here's my little secret, though: I love them even more when finished with apple cider vinegar while warm. So roast, transfer to a platter, and serve with a jug of vinegar just in case someone needs the extra tang.

SERVES 4

2 pounds Brussels sprouts, halved or quartered if large

4 garlic cloves, mashed

2 shallots, thinly sliced

3 tablespoons extra-virgin olive oil

Salt and freshly ground black pepper

Preheat the oven to 425°F. Line a baking sheet with parchment paper.

In a bowl, toss the Brussels sprouts, garlic, and shallots with the olive oil and season with salt and pepper. Arranged the tossed vegetables on the prepared baking sheet and roast until golden, about 30 minutes. Serve.

Poblano Rings

I REALLY THINK THIS IS ONE OF THE BEST DISHES I've ever come up with. Cut crosswise into rings, poblanos make for the perfect onion ring and a killer replacement for onions on your burger. I can eat a whole basket of these with just a mix of mayo and chipotle or even tartar sauce.

To char the poblanos, you might need to try it a couple of times before you master the technique. You're looking to char them completely, but if you overdo it, they might get too soft or disintegrate, making it hard to cut them into rings. In fact, for this recipe it's okay to undercook them slightly. Peel off as much of the char as you can, but it's fine and even adds flavor if you leave some of the charred bits.

SERVES 6

3 fresh poblano chiles

3 cups vegetable oil, or as needed, for frying

1 cup all-purpose flour

Salt

2 large eggs, beaten

2 cups panko bread crumbs

3 tablespoons ground dried guajillo chile or ground chipotle powder

Place the poblanos directly over a gas burner on medium-high heat. Using tongs, turn as needed so the chiles can char evenly. The chiles will turn black and look burned; this should not take more than 5 minutes because chiles can turn soft and release water if cooked for too long. Transfer the chiles to a resealable plastic bag and let steam for about 5 minutes. This will allow for easier peeling. Peel the charred skin off the chiles and slice into ¼-inch rings, discarding the stem.

Heat the vegetable oil in a large, heavy saucepan until a deep-fry thermometer inserted into the oil reaches 350°F. (If you do not have a thermometer, test the oil with a piece of bread crumb, which should sizzle when it touches the oil.)

Meanwhile, arrange three bowls in an assembly line: one of them with the all-purpose flour seasoned with about 1 teaspoon of salt, another one with the beaten eggs, and the third one with a mixture of the panko bread crumbs and ground guajillo.

Carefully dredge the poblano rings in the flour, making sure not to break them. Shake off the excess flour and soak in the beaten egg. Then cover with the panko-guajillo mixture.

Fry in the hot oil until crisp and golden in color, about 2 minutes. Remove from the oil and set on paper towels to drain the excess oil. Season with salt while the rings are still warm.

Roasted Nopales and Broccoli

NOPALES ARE CACTUS PADDLES, and we eat them for breakfast. They are slimy; it is what it is, and we love them. Nopales are usually chopped and cooked in boiling water to tenderize and remove that very sliminess, turning them an olive-green color. After that, they are tossed with a vinaigrette and maybe chopped tomatoes, onions, serranos, and some cilantro for a delectable salad with panela cheese. At Casa Marcela, I roast them. In Mexico, we are not roasters. The oven is seldom used—maybe for flan—but, for the most part, it's used for storage. Since moving to the U.S. side of the border, I find that roasting is now my favorite technique, especially for vegetables. My son Fausto absolutely loves nopales on the verge of being charred and sprinkled with lime juice, sea salt, and olive oil. In the market in Mexico, you can find them dehydrated (kind of like dehydrated mango), coated in chile-lime powder, and sold as candy. Super healthy and incredibly delicious!

SERVES 4

2 pounds nopales (cactus paddles), cleaned and cut into 2-inch strips

2 cups broccoli florets

3 tablespoons extra-virgin olive oil

Salt and freshly ground black pepper

½ lemon

Preheat the oven to 425°F. Line a baking sheet with parchment paper.

Spread the nopales strips and broccoli florets on the prepared baking sheet, drizzle with the olive oil, and season with salt and pepper. Toss to combine. Roast for 30 minutes, or until the veggies are golden brown. Squeeze the lemon half over the vegetables and serve.

Salsas

There might be a million different recipes for pico de gallo or salsa verde. You can, in fact, find plenty of those in my previous books. Here I offer you my favorites that are made at home, some weekly, some daily, and some only reserved for special occasions, but all are packed with flavor. What you need to understand about salsas are the chiles and what they add to your recipe. Some add spice, some add smoke, some add sweetness, and some add bitterness, and learning to combine them is one of the secrets of Mexican cuisine. All the salsas in this chapter are different but easy to prepare, and they use flavor combinations and ingredients that you are probably already familiar with. The idea is to try something new, something different.

Salsas make the dish. They do. They can take a bland piece of grilled fish and make it exquisite. Felipe cannot eat anything without nearly burning his tongue off with a chile. He needs the heat, as do a lot of folks who grew up in Mexico or with a Mexican *mamá* like he did. We just need flavor. We need that *sazón* in our dishes. Feel free to go the traditional route with a tomato-based pico, but here are some incredible and easy alternatives that are delicious and will surely wow your guests.

Chile de Árbol Peanut Butter

Crema de Cacahuate y Chile de Árbol

THIS IS NOT ONLY A GREAT SPREAD FOR BURRITOS but also a wonderful dipping sauce for apple or pear slices. As for the chiles, you get spice from the chile de árbol, as well as smoke and sweetness. Mexican chiles can be a little confusing to shop for because their names change depending on whether the chile is fresh or dried. A chile de árbol has the same name for the fresh and the dried version, but a chile guajillo is the dried version of a chile mirasol. Confusing, I know, but thank goodness for Google. Sometimes I even need to look them up to remind myself.

MAKES 1½ CUPS

2 cups unsalted peanuts

10 dried chiles de árbol, stemmed

1 dried guajillo chile, stemmed and seeded

8 garlic cloves

½ cup sunflower oil

1 tablespoon distilled white vinegar

Salt

Place the peanuts, chiles, and garlic in a food processor and process until a paste starts to form, about 2 minutes. Turn the machine off and add the oil and vinegar. Process until smooth, about 1 minute. Season to taste with salt.

Drunken Salsa with Mezcal

Salsa Borracha

BORRACHA MEANS "DRUNK," so any salsa with this word in the title means you're adding some sort of alcohol. It's usually either beer or tequila, but I wanted to try this with a smoky mezcal and loved the results. Serve this salsa with anything from grilled fish to carne asada tacos—any dish that needs a little kick.

MAKES 1½ CUPS

2 tablespoons extra-virgin olive oil

4 dried pasilla chiles, stemmed and seeded

½ cup mezcal

¼ cup freshly squeezed orange juice

½ cup chopped white onion

1 fresh serrano chile, stemmed

2 garlic cloves

Salt and freshly ground black pepper

1 teaspoon apple cider vinegar

Heat the olive oil in a medium sauté pan over medium heat. Add the pasilla chiles and fry until fragrant, 1 minute per side.

Transfer the chiles to a heavy medium pot, reserving the oil in the sauté pan. Add the mezcal and orange juice to the pot and bring to a boil. Decrease the heat and simmer for 5 minutes. Turn off the heat and let cool.

Meanwhile, reheat the oil in the sauté pan. Add the onion, serrano, and garlic and cook, stirring, until fragrant, about 5 minutes.

Transfer the pasilla and serrano mixtures to a blender and process until smooth. Stir in vinegar. Season to taste with salt and pepper.

Salsa Verde

THIS IS AN EASY SALSA THAT CAN BE USED for everything from enchiladas to dipping with homemade tortilla chips. I use serranos because I like the spice, but you could certainly use jalapeños instead. For the tomatillos, you'll know they are ready when they turn an olive-green color, which is when you need to stop cooking them; otherwise, they will burst and lose all of their juices from inside!

MAKES 3 CUPS

1½ pounds tomatillos, husked and rinsed

½ white onion

2 garlic cloves

1 serrano chile, stemmed, halved lengthwise

2 teaspoons salt, plus more to taste

¼ cup loosely packed fresh cilantro

Freshly ground black pepper

Bring 8 cups of water to a boil in a heavy medium pot. Add the tomatillos, onion, garlic, serrano chile, and salt. Cook until the tomatillos are dark green and the onion has softened, about 15 minutes. Using a slotted spoon to drain, transfer the salsa ingredients to a blender. Add the cilantro and process until smooth. Season to taste with salt and pepper.

Salsa de Molcajete

2 CUPS

3 tomatoes

2 fresh jalapeño chiles

2 dried chiles de árbol

2 garlic cloves, unpeeled

1 teaspoon kosher salt,
plus more to taste

In a cast-iron skillet over medium-high heat, dry-roast the tomatoes, jalapeños, chiles de árbol, and garlic. When the garlic's papery outer skin starts to brown, remove the garlic from the pan and carefully peel it, discarding the skin. Continue roasting the tomatoes, chiles, and jalapeños until soft and blackened on all sides. Transfer to a plate to cool.

Place the garlic in a molcajete (see headnote for Apple-Mint Lamb Chops, page 80) and season with the salt. Grind with the pestle until a paste forms. Add the chiles de árbol and grind until they break into tiny pieces. Stem the jalapeños before adding them to the molcajete. Grind the jalapeños. Add the tomatoes, one at a time, and grind until smooth. Season generously with salt. Serve warm, if desired.

Slightly cool the dry-roasted ingredients. Start by mashing the garlic until smooth. Add árbol chiles.

Grind the garlic, chiles de árbol, and salt to form a paste.

Stem the jalapeños before adding them to the molcajete. Grind the jalapeños. Add the ingredients with the most moisture at the end.

If you want a smoother salsa, keep grinding until the jalapeños are smooth.

Add the tomatoes, one at a time, and grind until smooth.

Continue adding tomatoes and grind into a chunky salsa.
Season with additional salt, if desired. Serve warm.

Morita, Guajillo, and Pasilla Chile Salsa

ALL-DRIED-CHILE SALSAS ARE MUCH SMOKIER and richer in flavor than their counterparts made with fresh chiles. Each chile in this salsa will give you something different. A *morita* is very spicy, similar to a serrano. The guajillo will give you tart-sweet notes, almost like berries or prunes. Pasillas are smoky, richly flavored, and more savory. First taste the salsa on its own and try to identify the flavors. Once you understand what each chile brings to the salsa, you can add or combine to your liking!

MAKES 2½ CUPS

1 tablespoon extra-virgin olive oil

2 dried guajillo chiles, stemmed, seeded

2 dried pasilla chiles, stemmed and seeded

2 dried morita chiles, stemmed and seeded

3 garlic cloves

1 tomato, cored and quartered

1 tomatillo, husked, rinsed, and halved

2 cups water

Salt and freshly ground black pepper

Heat the olive oil in a heavy medium sauté pan over medium-high heat. Add the chiles, garlic, tomato, and tomatillo and cook, stirring, until the chiles are soft and fragrant, about 5 minutes. Add the water and bring the mixture to a boil. Turn off the heat. Let cool slightly. Transfer the mixture to a blender and process until smooth. Season to taste with salt and pepper.

Pickled Red Onions

PICKLED RED ONIONS ARE GOOD with just about everything, including carnitas tacos, *cochinita pibil*, carne asada, grilled chicken, or even your sunny-side-up eggs in the morning. They add a vinegary kick that cuts fat and cools the palate.

MAKES 2 CUPS

1 red onion, quartered and cut into 1-inch strips

²⁄₃ cup freshly squeezed lime juice (from about 5 limes)

¼ cup extra-virgin olive oil

1 tablespoon crumbled dried oregano

1 teaspoon salt

Stir together all of the ingredients in a medium bowl. Let stand until the onions soften, about 30 minutes.

Habanero Crema (nondairy)

I WENT THROUGH A HABANERO CREMA PHASE. I did. I made a batch every few days and used it for everything from drizzling on tacos, to scrambling it into eggs, to using it as a base to make salad dressing (by blending in vinegar, avocado, and serrano chiles). I almost don't like the idea of labeling it a "crema" because, the truth is, no one likes substitutes. We like the real thing. And crema is crema, and nothing can replace that tangy rich perfection. But this here sauce is magnificent as just that. A sauce. You can play with consistency; sometimes I want it to be a little looser or a little thicker. And feel free to make it spicier.

It can also serve as a base to build on. Blend in canned chipotles in adobo, and serve as a dipping sauce for shrimp. Take out the habanero and lime juice and add honey, cinnamon, and lemon zest, and it's a dessert sauce to drizzle on pound cake and fresh mango slices. The possibilities are endless.

MAKES 3 CUPS

2 cups raw unsalted cashews, soaked in water for 3 hours and drained

1 fresh habanero chile, stemmed

1 tablespoon freshly squeezed lemon juice

¾ cup water

Salt and freshly ground black pepper

Combine the drained cashews and habanero chile in a food processor and pulse until a paste forms, scraping down the sides as needed. With the machine running, slowly add the lemon juice and water and blend until creamy, about 1 minute. Season to taste with salt and pepper.

You can play with the consistency of the crema by adding more liquid for a runnier crema or less than the stated amount to dollop like sour cream.

Avocado Crema

THE SECRET TO ANY GOOD AVOCADO-BASED RECIPE is knowing how to pick
a ripe avocado. Look for an avocado that, when gently pressed, gives to pressure
but is not too mushy or soft. Also, if the little round stem cannot be easily removed,
then it's not ready! If it's brown and easily rolls off, that's a good avocado.

All we're doing here is enhancing flavors of what, to me, is the
perfect fruit because of its flavor, texture, and nutritional value. In fact,
I prefer to eat avocados simply sliced, drizzled with olive oil, and sprinkled
with sea salt. But sometimes you need to be able to drizzle that avocado and
add some freshness to a tostada or a taco, so here you go.

MAKES 1¼ CUPS

1 cup firmly packed fresh
cilantro leaves

¾ cup Mexican crema

½ avocado, peeled and pitted

½ fresh jalapeño chile, stemmed

1 tablespoon freshly squeezed
lime juice

2 tablespoons water

Salt and freshly ground
black pepper

Combine the cilantro, Mexican crema, avocado, jalapeño, and lime juice
in a blender and process until smooth. Add the water and blend for
10 seconds. Season to taste with salt and pepper.

Pineapple, Morita, and Pine Nut Salsa

THIS SWEET, CREAMY SALSA IS GREAT WITH SEAFOOD. It's also delicious with something tangy, like a shrimp ceviche or Octopus Ceviche (page 5). Nut-based salsas are common in Mexico and are coarser and much thicker than fresh or even cooked salsas. They're almost like grainy nut butters. You can use this to spread or drizzle on tortillas, but I like to dip celery sticks and apple slices into it.

MAKES 1½ CUPS

3 garlic cloves, unpeeled

2 dried morita chiles, stemmed

½ cup pine nuts

3 tablespoons tequila reposado

1 (20-ounce) can pineapple slices, drained

Salt

Heat a dry, heavy skillet over medium heat. Add the garlic and chiles and toast, moving them continuously, until the chiles are soft, about 5 minutes. Add the pine nuts and toast until slightly golden, about 30 seconds (because of their high oil content, they burn very fast). Add the tequila and cook until slightly evaporated, about 1 minute. Turn off the heat. When the garlic is cool enough to handle, peel it. Transfer the ingredients to a blender. Add the pineapple and blend until smooth. Season to taste with salt.

Mint and Cilantro Salsa Verde

THIS SALSA SCREAMS FRESH and is a perfect pairing for Tacobab al Pastor (page 17) or Apple-Mint Lamb Chops (page 80). Salsas are not always tomato based, and this is a great one to try with dishes that aren't perhaps traditionally Mexican. I always have both fresh mint and fresh cilantro in the garden (me and my perfect California weather), and that certainly makes a difference in the sauce. People ask me all the time what I recommend planting in a container if they have no space for an ample garden, and these two herbs are at the top of my list. In fact, once mint catches on, it grows like crazy, so I actually keep it in a large pot and not in one of the beds, as I'm afraid it will take over (which wouldn't be horrible because thousands of mojitos are never a bad thing).

MAKES 1½ CUPS

2 cups firmly packed fresh cilantro leaves

1 cup firmly packed fresh mint leaves

¼ cup soy sauce

¼ cup distilled white vinegar

¼ cup extra-virgin olive oil

2 tablespoons honey

2 fresh jalapeño chiles, stemmed

Combine all of the ingredients in a blender and process until very smooth, about 1 minute. Serve immediately (if the salsa sits for too long, it will turn dark green because of the fresh herbs).

Salsa de Chile de Árbol

YES, YOU READ THE INGREDIENTS CORRECTLY—that's 60 chiles,
which may seem like a lot, but they get processed down to a yummy, spicy, smoky,
earthy salsa that's perfect for Tacos Dorados (page 18). This salsa is on
the spicy side, so be sure to let your family or guests know what's coming!

MAKES 1 CUP

2 tablespoons vegetable oil

60 dried chiles de árbol

5 garlic cloves, unpeeled

¼ cup chopped white onion

1 cup water

Salt

Heat the oil in a large, heavy skillet over medium-high heat. Add the chiles, garlic, and onion and cook, stirring continuously, until the chiles are toasted and fragrant, about 4 minutes. Remove from the heat. When the garlic is cool enough to handle, peel it. Transfer the ingredients to a food processor and add the water. Pulse until coarse and season to taste with salt. Serve.

Pickled Poblanos

YOU'VE PROBABLY NEVER THOUGHT OF PICKLING A POBLANO! Jalapeños are usually the pickled crowd favorite, but they can be spicy, so this is a milder version of a well-known garnish. Many salsas tend to separate after a few hours and so I suggest not making them ahead, but pickled poblanos will last for a good week and a half in your fridge! Double the recipe if you're feeding a group, and use this to complement any of your breakfast, lunch, or dinner dishes that need a vinegary kick.

MAKES 1½ CUPS

½ cup extra-virgin olive oil

¼ cup rice vinegar

3 tablespoons soy sauce

Juice of 1 orange

Juice of 1 lime

1 tablespoon vegetable oil

3 fresh poblano chiles,
cut into rings

½ white onion, cut into
½-inch slices

Whisk the olive oil, vinegar, soy sauce, orange juice, and lime juice together in a medium bowl until combined. Set aside.

Heat the vegetable oil in a large, heavy skillet over medium-high heat. Add the poblanos and onion and cook, stirring continuously, until fragrant and the poblanos are slightly soft, about 6 minutes. Add the orange-lime mixture and stir until well combined. Turn off the heat and let cool to room temperature before serving.

MERCADO HIDALGO IN TIJUANA

It's kind of crazy how normal it is for me to say, "Headed to the market, be back in a couple hours," and actually be referring to a market in, literally, another country. That's the life we live here on the border. There are certain ingredients I cannot find or prefer the Mexican version of, and for those, I head to the Mercado Hidalgo in Tijuana. You'd think it must be *some* tamarind paste if you have to cross an international border to get it but, with some ingredients, there's no comparison in both flavor and price. There's a catch, though . . . certain ingredients won't make it across the border. Generally, uncut fruit that still has seeds can't make it back into San Diego. The same for most cheeses for not being pasteurized. It is still worth the drive if only to enjoy the colorful scenery and sit down for a taco, torta, or a giant, warm piece of *chicharrón prenzado* (pork crackling) with lime juice and hot sauce. What can and does cross the border, though, are all of the Mexican candy, piñatas, and cooking/kitchen supplies that they sell like *molcajetes* and giant *ollas de tamal* (*tamal* pots). It's a gorgeous sight to see hundreds of types of chiles stacked up perfectly and all of the various types of *mole* pastes in crystal jugs ready to be packed and sold. While growing up in Tijuana, I used to go on Mondays with my mom. It's a fairly big market with multiple stands of each kind, but she always got her fruit, cheese, and candy from specific vendors. She knew them, and they knew her. She would get all that she could from the Mercado Hidalgo because of the cheaper prices. We'd go drop off everything at the house and head to the border to go into San Diego to buy the things that she preferred from the American supermarkets, like certain cheeses, pasta, cereals, and Twinkies! It's ironic that I do exactly the same thing now, only I reside on the U.S. side of the border!

Breakfast

Desayunos

The most important meal of the day. And, in Mexico, you don't rush out of the kitchen with a breakfast tart. Oh, no. You need to make sure you carve out a good hour of your day, because that's what chilaquiles or tamales or burritos deserve. Here you'll find mostly traditional breakfast items, along with one or two surprises. One of my favorite recipes in the book is the *huitlacoche*-based waffle batter in the Huitla Waffle (page 178).

For us, breakfast is a ritual, and often the only meal we have as a family, so we try to make the time to sit down and enjoy one another's company as well as the food. Some of the recipes are more labor-intensive, so they might be better for weekends, although the truth is most Mexican moms get up with the sun and start prepping tortillas for the *familia* while everybody else sleeps. I got in trouble once for saying that it's mostly the moms and women who cook on that side of the border. It's just fact. My father, for example, would sooner starve than go into the kitchen. Machismo? Sure. Was my mom a typical housewife? Not even close. She just happened to enjoy cooking, and when she couldn't (she had a medical condition that had her in bed a lot of the time) my dad had to hire a cook because he simply had no idea how to make anything at all. I think I once saw him go into the kitchen, starving, and all he came out with was a block of cheese and a knife. But the truth is, all the good recipes, the techniques, the secrets—they come from the *mujeres*. Here are mine for the best breakfasts you will serve your family yet.

Breakfast Skillet

Cazuela de Huevos y Nopales al Horno

NOPALES ARE CACTUS PADDLES, and I no longer have to steal them from a certain neighbor here in Chula Vista because I can now find them at my supermarket. It very well might be an acquired taste, as they tend to be on the slimy side, especially when served raw, but I grew up with them in everything from salads to quesadillas. Even though nopales have been a staple for centuries, they have become increasingly popular for their numerous health benefits. Cactus paddles have high amounts of soluble fiber, so they help fight high cholesterol. They're packed with vitamins (A, C, K, B_6), they're rich in antioxidants, and the list goes on. In Mexico, when you go on a diet, even your tortillas turn green! Tortillas made with cactus paddle masa are incredibly popular and now found nationwide.

SERVES 4

1 tablespoon salt, plus more to taste

4 cups 1-inch strips fresh nopales (spines removed)

¼ white onion

2 cups cored and coarsely chopped tomatoes

1 dried chile de árbol, stemmed

1 fresh serrano chile, stemmed

1 tomatillo, husked, rinsed, and halved

2 garlic cloves, mashed

Freshly ground black pepper

2 tablespoons vegetable oil

1½ cups ½-inch cubes peeled golden potatoes

4 large eggs

⅓ cup crumbled queso fresco

Fresh cilantro leaves, for garnish

Avocado slices, for serving

Crispy baguette, for serving

Preheat the broiler on high.

Bring 8 cups of water plus the 1 tablespoon of salt to a boil in a large, heavy pot. Add the nopales and onion and cook until tender, about 7 minutes. Drain.

Transfer the cooked onion to a blender and add the tomatoes, chile de árbol, serrano chile, tomatillo, and garlic and process until smooth. Season to taste with salt and pepper.

Heat the vegetable oil in a cast-iron skillet over medium-high heat. Add the potatoes and cook until crisp, about 3 minutes per side. Pour the tomato sauce over the potatoes and bring to a boil. Decrease to a simmer and cook for about 6 minutes. Add the drained nopales and cook until the flavors blend, about 2 more minutes.

Crack the eggs on top of the potato and nopales mixture and season with salt and pepper. Transfer the skillet to the oven and broil until the eggs are cooked, about 5 minutes.

Crumble the queso fresco on top of the cooked eggs and sprinkle with cilantro leaves. Serve with the avocado slices and a crispy baguette for dipping in the sauce.

Chorizo and Egg Burritos

Burritos de Huevo con Chorizo

CHORIZO IS AN INTERESTING TOPIC when cooking Mexican food outside of Mexico. It seems that the flavor that I grew up with has yet to be replicated for the American market (working on it!), but here's what I look for: a bright-red soft chorizo that needs to be pushed out of the casing and into the pan. It needs to have plenty of fat—in fact, so much that you might have to remove some after rendering. It tends to clump up, so use the back of a wooden spoon to break it up while stirring and cooking. There is nothing quite like the smell of chorizo to get you out of bed. These burritos are simple but loaded with flavor and a favorite way to start the day. If you want to pack them in your or your kids' lunch, wrap them in parchment paper first and then in foil. That will keep them warm without getting soggy. Use the same method if you want to freeze them, but let them cool first.

MAKES 8 BURRITOS

1 tablespoon vegetable oil

2 cups ⅛-inch cubes peeled russet potatoes

6 ounces fresh pork chorizo, casing removed

½ cup diced white onion

5 large eggs

8 flour tortillas, warmed

Heat the vegetable oil in a large, heavy skillet over medium-high heat. Add the potatoes and cook, moving them continuously, until golden brown and cooked through, about 6 minutes. Add the chorizo and cook, breaking it up with a spatula, until crisp, about 5 minutes. Add the onion and cook, stirring, until fragrant, about 3 minutes longer.

Whisk the eggs in a medium bowl and stir into the chorizo mixture. Cook, stirring, until the eggs are scrambled and just set, about 6 minutes. Turn off the heat.

Divide the mixture among the warmed tortillas and fold into burritos. Serve warm.

Scrambled Eggs with Onion, Tomato, and Chile

Huevos a la Mexicana con Jamón

THIS IS A SIMPLE, HOMESTYLE BREAKFAST that I had very often growing up in Tijuana. Instead of serving it with tortillas, though, I like it with a buttered piece of toast for between bites of the scrambled egg. In fact, I would challenge myself while eating this; I would make sure that the last bite of scrambled egg would coincide with the last bite of toast. A little obsessive-compulsive but a great memory nonetheless. Pickled jalapeños are the spicy kick of choice.

SERVES 4

1 tablespoon vegetable oil

1 cup diced white onion

1 cup diced ham

1 cup diced tomato

1 fresh serrano chile, stemmed and minced

Salt and freshly ground black pepper

4 large eggs

2 tablespoons chopped fresh cilantro leaves

Heat the vegetable oil in a large, heavy skillet over medium-high heat. Add the onion and cook, stirring continuously, until translucent, about 4 minutes. Add the ham, tomato, and serrano chile and cook, stirring, until fragrant, about 6 minutes. Season to taste with salt and pepper.

Whisk the eggs together in a medium bowl and stir into the vegetable mixture. Cook, stirring, until the eggs are scrambled and just set, about 6 minutes. Taste and adjust the seasonings. Turn off the heat. Top with the cilantro and serve immediately.

"No confundas las enchiladas con los chilaquiles."

Chipotle and Shredded-Chicken Chilaquiles

Chilaquiles de Pollo al Chipotle

WE ALL KNOW AND LOVE CHILAQUILES, but perhaps not chipotle chilaquiles. They are a little spicier and smokier than the traditional, though certainly delicious. The trick to chilaquiles is to get them crispy but not burn them. Although I do say to fry until "lightly brown," make sure the tortillas are very crisp so that they have some bite when you add the sauce. It's about preference. What's universal is that adding the chipotle and then topping with fresh crema is the perfect combination.

SERVES 4

2 pounds Roma tomatoes, halved

1 white onion, halved

3 garlic cloves, unpeeled

3 tablespoons extra-virgin olive oil

4 teaspoons salt, plus more to taste

2 boneless, skinless chicken breasts (about 6 ounces each)

Freshly ground black pepper

½ cup low-sodium chicken broth

1 canned chipotle chile in adobo sauce plus 1 tablespoon of the sauce

⅓ cup vegetable oil

10 corn tortillas, cut into eighths, preferably stale (spread out to dry overnight)

½ cup crumbled cotija cheese

2 thin slices onion, separated into rings

½ cup Mexican crema, crème fraîche, or sour cream

¼ cup chopped fresh cilantro leaves, for garnish

Preheat the oven to 400°F. Line a baking sheet with aluminum foil.

Place the tomatoes, onion halves, and garlic on half of the prepared baking sheet, drizzle with 2 tablespoons of the olive oil, and season with 2 teaspoons of the salt. Toss to combine. Place the chicken breasts on the other half of the same pan, drizzle with the remaining 1 tablespoon olive oil, and season with the remaining 2 teaspoons salt and some pepper. Roast until the tomatoes are slightly charred and the chicken is cooked through, about 45 minutes. Remove from the oven and let cool.

When cool enough to handle, peel the garlic. Transfer the tomatoes, onion, and peeled garlic to a blender and add the chicken broth, chipotle chile, and adobo sauce. Blend until smooth, about 1 minute. Taste and adjust the seasonings with salt and pepper.

After letting them cool for a bit, place the chicken breasts on a work surface and shred, using two forks or your fingers, into 1-inch pieces.

Meanwhile, pour the vegetable oil into a large sauté pan over medium heat. When the oil is hot, add the tortilla pieces, working in two or three batches, and cook until lightly browned on both sides and crisp, about 3 minutes per side. Drain the tortillas on paper towels and discard the remaining oil. Wipe the pan with a paper towel.

In the same pan, bring the salsa from the blender to a simmer over low heat. Add the shredded chicken and fried tortillas and cook until soft but not mushy, about 5 minutes. Season with salt and pepper to taste. Divide the mixture among four individual dishes. Top with the cheese and onion rings. Drizzle with the crema, sprinkle with some chopped fresh cilantro, and serve immediately.

Fruit Salad with Cottage Cheese

Ensalada de Frutas

IT'S KIND OF AMAZING that this incredibly popular breakfast fruit salad
is available in practically every corner of Mexico but has never made its way
to the United States. I go to this little place called Papayas in my Chula Vista
neighborhood to find it, but it's not really a popular dish outside of the Mexican
communities and restaurants. Maybe it's the combination of cottage cheese and fruit.
I find it absolutely delightful along with the sweet honey and crunchy granola.

SERVES 6

GRANOLA

2 cups old-fashioned oats
(not quick-cooking)

½ cup sliced almonds

½ cup coarsely chopped hazelnuts

¼ cup dried cranberries

¼ cup dark raisins

¼ cup unsweetened
shredded coconut

1 teaspoon ground cinnamon

¼ teaspoon salt

¼ cup lightly packed
light brown sugar

¼ cup honey

4 tablespoons (½ stick)
unsalted butter

1 teaspoon pure vanilla extract

FRUIT SALAD

1 cup diced (1½-inch cubes) melon

1 cup diced (1½-inch cubes)
watermelon

1 cup diced (1½-inch cubes)
pineapple

1 cup quartered strawberries

1 cup diced (1½-inch cubes)
papaya

1 (16-ounce) container
cottage cheese

½ cup pumpkin seeds, for serving

½ cup unsweetened shredded
coconut, for serving

Honey, for serving

Preheat the oven to 400°F. Line a baking sheet with parchment paper and set aside.

For the granola, mix the oats, almonds, hazelnuts, cranberries, raisins, coconut, cinnamon, and salt in a medium bowl.

Combine the brown sugar, honey, and butter in a medium saucepan over medium heat, stirring until the butter melts and the mixture begins to boil. Add the vanilla and stir. Remove from the heat.

Pour the butter over the oats, mixing until well coated. Transfer to the prepared pan and, using a spatula, press the oats evenly into the pan. Bake for 20 to 25 minutes, or until the top is golden brown. Transfer to a rack and let cool. Using the parchment paper as an aid, lift out of the pan and place on a work surface. Crumble into pieces.

For the fruit salad, combine the diced fruit in a large bowl and mix to combine. Divide among six serving dishes and top with the cottage cheese, crumbled granola, pumpkin seeds, shredded coconut, and honey.

CASA MARCELA

Aztec Fruit Bars

I TRAVEL A LOT. When I have time, I like to pack my lunches, and these are
a great energy source when on the run. The "Aztec" part comes from the amaranth,
an ingredient they used and prized for its nutritional value. It was even part of
Mayan religious rituals. In Mexico, it's mostly found in candy bars called *alegrías*,
which is sweetened, popped amaranth. I made them more into a breakfast bar.
You need to pop the amaranth in a dry skillet just like you would pop corn kernels.
Follow the package instructions and use ¼ cup for this recipe, and the
remainder you can use to sprinkle on salads or even use as a crust on fish.

MAKES 16 BARS

⅓ cup all-purpose flour

2 teaspoons ancho chile powder

¼ teaspoon salt

⅛ teaspoon baking soda

⅛ teaspoon baking powder

1 cup chopped raw almonds

¾ cup quartered dried apricots

½ cup dried cranberries

½ cup quartered dried figs

½ cup pitted and quartered dates

½ cup chopped
bittersweet chocolate

⅓ cup packed light brown sugar

¼ cup popped amaranth
(see headnote)

1 large egg

1 tablespoon honey

½ teaspoon pure vanilla extract

Preheat the oven to 325°F and place the rack in the center of the oven.
Line an 8 x 8-inch baking pan with aluminum foil and set aside.

In a large bowl, whisk together the flour, ancho chile powder, salt,
baking soda, and baking powder. Stir in the almonds, dried fruit, bittersweet chocolate, brown sugar, and popped amaranth. Use your fingers to
make sure that everything has been coated with the flour mixture evenly.

In the bowl of a stand mixer fitted with the whisk attachment, beat
the egg, honey, and vanilla until thick, about 1 minute. Add the egg
mixture to the fruit mixture and stir, using a spatula, until everything is
coated. Spread into the prepared baking pan, pressing to even out.

Bake for about 30 minutes, or until the top is golden brown and the
edges have pulled away from the sides of the pan. Remove from the oven
and let cool. When cooled, lift the bar from the pan by the edges of the
aluminum foil. Use a sharp knife to cut into 16 even squares.

Huitla Waffle

WHEN OUT AND ABOUT EATING, I'm always imagining in my head how adding this chile or that Mexican herb could turn an existing classic into a new and exciting dish. Here, a few different dynamics collide. *Huitlacoche*, considered a delicacy in Mexico, has a wonderful smoky and mushroomy flavor that is one of my overall favorites in the Mexican kitchen, and is usually reserved for quesadillas or crepes. Well, I mixed it into my waffle batter along with some chives and then dressed it like eggs Benedict. Oddly enough, this is one of my favorite recipes in the book while having zero Mexican tradition or history attached. It's all Casa Marcela.

SERVES 2

1 (7-ounce) can huitlacoche (undrained)

¾ cup whole milk

1 cup store-bought pancake mix (the kind that only requires oil and a liquid to be mixed in, no eggs)

5 tablespoons chopped fresh chives

2 tablespoons extra-virgin olive oil

Salt

2 large eggs

½ cup Mexican crema

¼ cup drained capers, plus more for garnish

Freshly ground black pepper

6 thin slices smoked salmon

1 tablespoon chopped fresh dill

1 tablespoon fresh cilantro leaves

Put the huitlacoche and milk in a blender and blend until smooth. Pour into a large bowl and add the pancake mix, 2 tablespoons of the chives, 1 tablespoon of the olive oil, and a pinch of salt.

Heat a waffle iron on medium. Cook half of the batter in the waffle iron until cooked through. Repeat with the remaining batter.

Meanwhile, heat the remaining 1 tablespoon olive oil in a saucepan over medium heat, crack in the eggs, and cook sunny-side up.

In another small bowl, combine 2 tablespoons of the chives, the crema, and ¼ cup capers. Season to taste with salt and pepper.

Place 1 huitla waffle on a plate. Top with 3 slices of the smoked salmon and 1 egg. Drizzle with the chive crema and sprinkle with some of the remaining chives. Repeat with the remaining waffle, egg, chive crema, and capers. Top both waffles with dill and cilantro leaves.

Bizcochuelos with Thyme-Piloncillo Butter

BIZCOCHUELOS (BREAD ROLLS) WERE MADE on ranches here in California for either breakfast or dessert, usually using Grandma's recipe that was handed down from generation to generation. You can serve these for breakfast but they would also make a great addition to your Thanksgiving table. Piloncillo is unrefined whole cane sugar found in a cone shape throughout Mexico or in a Hispanic market. It can be very hard or somewhat soft, depending on the moisture content. If it's a really hard cone, it's more of a scrape (with your knife) than a chop. Although there is no flavor that can compare to the deep, rich, molassesy taste of piloncillo, dark brown sugar is a good substitute.

MAKES 20 BUNS

THYME-PILONCILLO BUTTER

8 tablespoons (1 stick) unsalted butter, at room temperature

3 tablespoons minced piloncillo

1 tablespoon finely chopped fresh thyme

½ teaspoon kosher salt

BIZCOCHUELOS

1 (2¼-teaspoon) package active dry yeast

¾ cup plus 1 teaspoon granulated sugar

¾ cup lukewarm water (110°F)

4 large eggs, plus 1 large egg, beaten

1 teaspoon salt

4 cups all-purpose flour, plus ¾ cup for kneading

8 tablespoons (1 stick) unsalted butter, at room temperature, plus extra for brushing

CINNAMON SUGAR

½ cup granulated sugar

1 teaspoon ground cinnamon

Honey, for serving

For the thyme-piloncillo butter, place the butter in a medium bowl. Add the piloncillo, thyme, and salt and mix well. Place on a sheet of parchment paper and roll up into a log. Chill until firm, about 1 hour.

For the bizcochuelos, in a large bowl, combine the active dry yeast, 1 teaspoon of the granulated sugar, and the lukewarm water and let stand until foamy, about 10 minutes. Add the remaining ¾ cup granulated sugar, 4 eggs, and salt and whisk until well combined. Add 1 cup of the flour and the softened butter while whisking, until fully incorporated. Add 3 cups of the flour and continue to mix. The dough will be sticky. Transfer the dough to a floured surface and knead, adding the remaining ¾ cup flour as needed, for about 6 minutes. Brush the butter over the dough and let it rest in a covered bowl until doubled in size, about 2 hours. Divide the dough into 20 equal balls and place on a baking sheet. Let rest for 45 minutes more.

Meanwhile, preheat the oven 350°F.

For the cinnamon sugar, combine the sugar and cinnamon in a small bowl. Brush the beaten egg on top of each bun and sprinkle 1 teaspoon of the cinnamon-sugar mixture on top.

Bake until golden brown, 20 to 25 minutes. Let cool and serve with the thyme-piloncillo butter and honey.

Conchas

CONCHAS ARE NAMED AFTER THE SHAPE of their sugar topping, which resembles a seashell. I never really thought about making these at home because I had *panaderías* (pastry shops) on every corner in Tijuana growing up. My absolute favorite way to eat these is to top them with a very large pat of butter and then pop in the oven (or microwave) to melt the butter into the sugary topping and into the bread. Felipe, *el novio*, likes to dunk it into his coffee or hot chocolate in the morning. In fact, we just recently stayed at La Esperanza resort in Cabo and we had to limit his *concha* intake. The man could start the day with an entire basket of *conchas*.

MAKES 10 CONCHAS

CONCHAS

½ cup lukewarm water (110°F)

2 tablespoons instant dry yeast

¾ cup plus 1 tablespoon granulated sugar

3½ cups all-purpose flour, plus ¼ cup for dusting

4 large eggs, slightly whisked

½ teaspoon salt

3 tablespoons unsalted butter, at room temperature

1½ teaspoons extra-virgin olive oil

SUGAR TOPPING

1 cup all-purpose flour

1 cup confectioners' sugar

8 tablespoons (1 stick) unsalted butter

2 tablespoons unsweetened cocoa powder

For the conchas, in a large bowl, combine the warm water, yeast, and 1 tablespoon of the granulated sugar. Let stand until foamy, about 10 minutes.

Place the 3½ cups of the flour on a clean work surface and make a well in the center. Pour in the yeast mixture, eggs, remaining ¾ cup sugar, and salt. Combine, using your fingers, and mix until it starts to come together (the dough will be very sticky; use the remaining ¼ cup flour and a dough scraper to help you knead until you have a well-formed ball of dough).

Add the butter and knead until elastic and very smooth, about 10 minutes. Grease a large bowl with the olive oil and place the dough in the bowl. Cover with plastic wrap and let rise for about 1 hour.

Place the risen dough on a lightly floured surface and divide into twelve 2-inch balls, each about 3½ ounces. Roll each ball under your palm.

Place the dough balls on a greased baking sheet, cover with plastic, and let rise until doubled in size, about 1 hour.

For the sugar topping, while the dough is rising, combine the flour, confectioners' sugar, and butter in a large bowl and mix with your hands until a moist dough forms. Divide the sugar dough in half and add the cocoa powder to one half. Continue to mix until the cocoa is completely incorporated. Use 1 tablespoon of the sugar topping, flattened into a ¼-inch-thick disk, to cover each concha (you will have 6 chocolate conchas and 6 vanilla conchas). It should cover most of the surface.

Cut through the sugar topping with a sharp knife, making diagonal lines or any decoration that reminds you of a shell. Flatten each concha slightly and let rise for 1 hour longer.

Preheat the oven to 375°F.

Bake the conchas for 20 minutes, or until golden on the edges and puffed up.

"Las penas con pan
son buenas."

Mantecadas

THIS RECIPE IS INSPIRED BY traditional *mantecadas*, but I always
thought they were too greasy, so I made this recipe a little more "cakey."
They are great with a cup of hot chocolate or some jam.

MAKES 18

1½ cups all-purpose flour

1 tablespoon baking powder

½ teaspoon salt

6 tablespoons (¾ stick)
unsalted butter

1 cup granulated sugar

4 large eggs

⅓ cup whole milk

1 teaspoon pure vanilla extract

18 red paper cupcake liners

Preheat the oven to 425°F. Line 18 cups of two standard muffin tins with paper liners.

Put the flour, baking powder, and salt in a medium bowl and whisk until combined. Set aside.

Beat the butter and sugar in the bowl of a stand mixer until well blended, about 3 minutes. Add the eggs and mix until fluffy, about 2 minutes more. Add the milk and vanilla and mix to combine. Add the flour mixture in three batches, making sure to blend well after each addition.

Divide the batter among the cupcake liners and bake for 5 minutes. Lower the oven temperature to 375°F and bake until golden, about 10 minutes longer. Let cool and then turn them out onto a serving platter.

"Cásate con una que sepa cocinar, la belleza se acaba pero el hambre no..."

Tamales de Pollo en Salsa Verde

DON'T BE AFRAID OF TAMALES. Once you master the masa, they are a breeze to make, though some would argue that perfecting masa-making technique takes decades. I give you amounts, but it's about how the masa feels in your hand. I have no idea of the temperature or humidity in your kitchen, so the water/broth measure may vary. The thing is, the masa needs to be soft but spreadable, and light and fluffy, not dense. Vivi, my former assistant whom you can see in these gorgeous photos, has been making tamales with her mother and grandmother since she was a little girl. And even though I'd been making tamales for a while, it was not until watching her that I really mastered the masa.

MAKES 12 TO 14 TAMALES

MASA

1 cup lard

2 cups dry masa harina

2 teaspoons salt

1 teaspoon baking powder

1⅓ cups chicken broth

GREEN CHICKEN FILLING

1 (1-pound) boneless, skinless chicken breast

3 garlic cloves

2 dried bay leaves

8 tomatillos (about 1 pound), husked and rinsed

2 jalapeño chiles, stemmed

¼ onion

¼ cup loosely packed fresh cilantro leaves

2 tablespoons vegetable oil

Salt

14 corn husks, soaked in water overnight

For the masa, place the lard in the bowl of a stand mixer fitted with the paddle attachment and beat on medium speed until light and fluffy, about 5 minutes. Add the masa harina and beat for 2 minutes more. Add the salt and baking powder and beat for about 5 minutes. Add the broth and beat until the masa is soft and fluffy (the masa should come off the sides of the bowl easily). Set aside, cover with a damp towel, and let rest for about 10 minutes, or until ready to use.

For the green chicken filling, place the chicken, garlic, and bay leaves in a medium pot and cover with water. Bring to a boil, decrease the heat to medium, and simmer until the chicken is cooked through, about 30 minutes. Remove from the heat and set aside until cool enough to handle. Remove the chicken breast from the pot and shred with two forks or your fingers. Set aside.

To the same pan of water, add the tomatillos, jalapeños, and onion and cook, stirring, until the tomatillos are dark green, about 20 minutes. Transfer the tomatillos, jalapeños, onion, and garlic to a blender and add the cilantro and ½ cup cooking liquid from the chicken. Blend until smooth.

Heat the vegetable oil in a medium pan and add the shredded chicken. Cook, stirring, for 1 minute, and then add the green salsa. Cook until the flavors are blended, about 5 minutes. Taste and adjust the seasonings with salt.

To fill the tamales, hold an opened, softened corn husk in one hand and spread about 1½ tablespoons of the dough on the husk, beginning 1 inch from the wider top and ending at least 1½ inches from the narrower bottom, leaving a 1½-inch border on either side. Sprinkle about 1½ tablespoons of the filling down the center of the dough. Fold the sides of the husk up and over the filling, tucking the ends under. Repeat with the remaining dough and filling.

Place the folded tamales in the steamer basket of a large pot. Add enough water to cover the bottom of the pot by several inches, but not enough to touch the tamales themselves. Bring to a boil, cover with a towel and a lid, decrease the heat to medium-low, and steam for 2 hours, adding more water to the pot as necessary. Do not allow the pot to boil dry. Open a tamal after 1 hour and check for doneness. The tamales should be firm and pull away from the husks without sticking. If still sticky, continue steaming until done.

"El que nace
pa'tamal del cielo
le caen las hojas."

Place lard in the bowl of a mixer and beat for 5 minutes on medium speed, or until lard is light and fluffy.

Add masa harina and beat for 2 minutes more.

Add baking powder and salt. Continue beating for about 5 minutes until well incorporated.

Add broth and continue to beat until masa is soft and fluffy.

Continue to beat until masa is spreadable but comes off the bowl easily.

Set aside, cover with a damp towel to prevent drying and let rest for about 10 minutes, or until ready to use.

Holding an open, softened corn husk in one hand, spread about 1½ tablespoons of the dough on the husk beginning 1 inch from the wider top and ending at least 1 ½ inches from the narrower bottom, leaving a 1½-inch border on either side.

Spread about 1½ tablespoons of filling down the center of each tamal.

Spread the filling to cover almost all of the masa.

Fold the sides of the husk up and over the filling, to cover a little more than half of it.

Fold the bottom third of the husk up and over to secure the bottom half of the tamal.

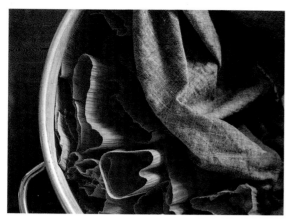

Place the folded tamales in the steamer basket of a large pot. Add enough water to fill the pot by several inches, but not enough to touch the tamales themselves. Bring to a boil, cover with towel and lid, and steam over medium-low heat for 2 hours, adding additional water to the pot as necessary. Do not allow pot to boil dry.

Open a tamal after 1 hour and check for doneness. The tamales should be firm and pull away from the husks without sticking. If still sticky, continue steaming until done. Allow to cool slightly before serving.

Pineapple Tamales

THESE TAMALES ARE sweet, soft, billowy perfection. I ate six of these
when we made them, popping them in my mouth like Tic Tacs. The sweet
variety of tamales are mostly reserved for breakfast, but these are
amazing any time of the day (or night). The pineapple not only adds sweetness
and flavor but also tenderizes the masa. As with any *tamal*, make a huge batch,
cool, and freeze, and then add to the steamer as many as you need at a time.

MAKES 12 TO 14 TAMALES

PILONCILLO SYRUP

4 ounces piloncillo

1 cup water

MASA

1 cup lard

2 cups masa harina

2 teaspoons salt

1 teaspoon baking powder

1½ cups crushed pineapple

½ cup dark raisins

1 teaspoon ground cinnamon

14 corn husks, soaked in water
overnight

For the piloncillo syrup, combine the piloncillo and water in a small
saucepan and cook over medium-high heat until the piloncillo is completely dissolved, about 10 minutes; there is no need to stir. Remove from
the heat and let cool slightly.

For the masa, place the lard in the bowl of a stand mixer fitted with
the paddle attachment and beat until light and fluffy, about 5 minutes.
Add the masa harina and beat for 2 minutes more. Add the salt and baking powder and beat for 5 minutes. Starting with the piloncillo syrup and
finishing with the pineapple, add the syrup and pineapple in alternating
batches and continue to beat until the masa is soft and fluffy. Add the
raisins and cinnamon and mix until well incorporated (the masa should
come off the sides of the bowl easily). Set aside, cover with a damp towel,
and let rest for about 10 minutes, or until ready to use.

To fill the tamales, tear pieces of the corn husks to create about
30 pieces of string.

Holding an opened, softened corn husk in one hand, spread about
1½ tablespoons of the dough on the husk, beginning 1 inch from the wider
top and ending at least 1½ inches from the narrower bottom, leaving a
1½-inch border on either side. Roll up loosely, like a cigar, and tie both ends
with husk string like you would candy. Continue with the remaining masa.

Place the folded tamales in the steamer basket of a large pot. Add
enough water to cover the bottom of the pot by several inches, but not
enough to touch the tamales themselves. Bring to a boil, cover with a
towel and a lid, decrease the heat to medium-low, and steam for
2½ hours, adding more water to the pot as necessary. Do not allow the
pot to boil dry. Open a tamal after 1 hour and check for doneness. The
tamales should be firm and pull away from the husks without sticking.
If still sticky, continue steaming until done.

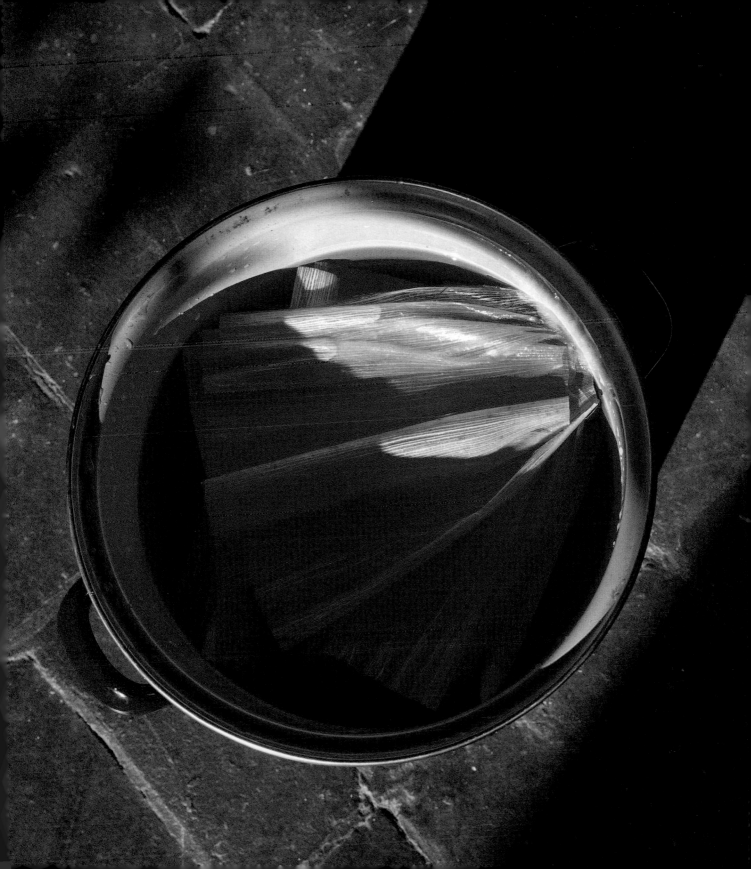

SOME THOUGHTS FROM
THE DESIGNER OF MY HOME, KARI ARENDSEN

I first met Marcela on a retreat in 2011, and we just clicked right away. We stayed in touch in the following years, and when Marcela purchased the Cook House, she reached out to me to discuss the interior design. Marcela is a strong, creative woman with an unmistakable aesthetic. Though she is known for her ability to help foodies prepare traditional Mexican fare with ease, she has a broad range of tastes and interests. In her day-to-day world, how she cooks is how she lives—infusing diverse classical styles with traditional Mexican themes. After collaborative discussions to develop the concept, "Euro-Mexa" became the driving theme behind the design. It was a direction I felt very comfortable with.

Growing up in a bilingual household that embraced Mexican culture, I already had a profound love for the people and places that represent its essence. Additionally, like Marcela's time in Paris studying French pastry, I spent my formative years as a designer in the City of Light. The beauty of the old world architecture, the ivy-covered buildings, and the cozy outdoor cafés all combined to imbue me with a deep sense of love and happiness for classical European design. It all brought back beautiful memories of being a child surrounded by the antiques and collectables that filled my grandparent's home. Each object transcended the physical with their own incredible stories and meanings. To this day I feel there is no room for

ordinary meaningless "stuff" taking up space in any interior we design at ILI. Through my friendship with Marcela I already knew she felt the same way. But ultimately, it was the home itself that was the main character in this production.

The spaces we live in have a profound effect on our well-being. Colors, textures, and materials are just some of the tangible elements that affect how we feel in our daily lives. For Marcela we curated elements that would anchor each space in the home while embracing and enhancing the lifestyle of this busy, creative, and always-innovating chef. The furnishings had to be relevant today, while simultaneously respecting the integrity of this historical home and ultimately withstanding the test of time and tastes. We selected and integrated large pieces from sofas to dining tables, more permanent pieces like window treatments and wallpaper, and functional elements like unique plumbing fixtures and custom closets. Everything we did had to honor both the home and its inhabitants. Collaborating with such an inspiring client, I think it's safe to say we were successful in achieving this goal.

So much more could be written here, but alas I only have a few paragraphs. I am over the moon to have been a part of bringing this home to life for Marcela and her family. To have played a supporting role in the joy this home brings to them is something I will always treasure. Thank you, Marcela.

Drinks

Bebidas

If this chapter was an honest assessment of what exists in my bar, all you would find is a really good tequila bottle, some perfectly ripe orange wedges, and some really good French wines. That's it. That's not just for weekend drinking, that's for all-week drinking. Felipe, *el fiancé*, and I really enjoy our time at the table together with the kids, and a healthy introduction to alcohol is, personally, very important to me. In moderation, a good pairing can bring a piece of meat to a whole new level. After a long day, just a couple ounces of a good reposado can really help the body just soften up and sink into the chair at the dinner table. So, why all these mixed drinks, you ask? Well, because they're not only delicious, they can save you a whole bunch of money and planning when you're entertaining. I would never, ever suggest a subpar tequila, even if it's for a mixed drink. I can taste everything. I get funny looks from bartenders when I ask for margaritas on the rocks with a 1942 but, listen, tequila is like oxygen where I'm from. Wrong kind or wrong dose and you die. So making a delicious mix to stretch it a little is a great solution when you have a gathering with friends or family. Also, most people don't drink alcohol straight (who are these people?) so you'd also have to worry about mixers. And who's gonna mix all those drinks? Not me. I'll be drinking tequila and eating cheese.

Now, a quick lesson on how you (should) drink tequila. You could actually drink it any way you darn well please, depending on your motivation. If the motivation is to wake up in an unknown location, then move along. It's valid, just not how I roll (at least not anymore, ha!). If the motivation is to truly savor and understand the drink, then do it like my dad. Pop an orange in the fridge the night before, and cut it into wedges. (Not rings. I hate orange rings. That's what they always give me at bars, and I'm always tempted to just drive around town with oranges and a paring knife in my handbag in case of emergencies.) Pour yourself the equivalent of a shot or two of tequila in a small snifter (cognac glass or balloon). I prefer the smaller ones, five-and-a-half ounces, because I'm a tiny person and don't drink much, but it's perfectly acceptable to use regular size glasses. Just please don't fill them, or you'll end up in the hospital. Then, put on some Luis Miguel or Frank Sinatra or, even better, a duet of the two, and take small bites of the orange wedge between tequila sips. Which tequila, you ask? The good kind. Whether you prefer blanco, reposado, añejo, or extra-añejo is up to you (and a two-second Google search will tell you the difference in aging). Price is certainly a good indicator. Just make sure somewhere on the label it says 100% blue agave. I prefer agaves grown in the highlands of Jalisco, which should also be mentioned somewhere on the label.

Either way, good alcohol makes for good drinks, mixed or not. And the best little tidbit of information you might get from this book? Here it goes: The cleaner the alcohol, the smaller the hangover. Yup. It was both a wonderful and terrible day when I realized I wouldn't wake up looking and feeling like the exorcist if I stuck to straight reposado and orange wedges all night. Clean alcohol and minimal sugar . . . you're welcome.

Mexican Mule

EVERY RESTAURANT I VISIT NOWADAYS has some sort of Moscow Mule on their cocktail menu. I'm not a huge vodka drinker, but I do love how it is served in those gorgeous copper mugs, so I thought to myself, "I need to whip this up with tequila." If you have those copper mugs, use them for this. The metal keeps the cocktail cold for a very long time.

SERVES 4

½ fresh serrano chile, stemmed

½ cup granulated sugar

½ cup water

¼ cup loosely packed fresh mint leaves, plus more for garnish

½ cup tequila blanco

¼ cup freshly squeezed lime juice

1 (12-ounce) bottle ginger beer, chilled

Combine the serrano chile, sugar, water, and mint in a small, heavy pot. Stir over medium heat until the sugar dissolves, about 2 minutes. Remove from the heat and let cool completely. Once the simple syrup is cooled, discard the serrano.

In a large pitcher, combine the tequila, lime juice, and cooled simple syrup. Stir to combine.

Fill four glasses with ice cubes. Divide the tequila mixture among them. Top with the ginger beer and garnish with mint leaves. Serve immediately.

Hibiscus Mimosas

Mimosas de Jamaica

AGUA DE JAMAICA IS SERVED in every single Mexican household, and every household has its own way of preparing it. There is no actual recipe for it because it is composed of three ingredients and three ingredients only: water, hibiscus flowers, and sugar. That's it. This recipe is absolutely stunning and highlights the beauty of the hibiscus flower with the syrup and the delicious powdered rim. It is perfect to serve at a party the moment guests walk in the door. In my version, it is very refreshing and crisp with the sparkling wine yet sweet and tangy with the flavor of hibiscus. Serve in champagne flutes for an elegant touch.

SERVES 6

2 cups water

¾ cup dried hibiscus flowers

½ cup granulated sugar

Pinch of salt

1 lime, cut into wedges

1 (750-ml) bottle white sparkling wine, chilled

Bring the water to a boil in a large, heavy pot. Add ½ cup of the hibiscus flowers, lower the heat, and simmer for 5 minutes. Remove from the heat and let steep for 10 minutes. Strain through a fine-mesh strainer, reserving the liquid, and let cool.

Meanwhile, put the remaining ¼ cup dried hibiscus flowers in a spice grinder and process until finely ground. Combine with ¼ cup of the sugar and a pinch of salt and place on a small plate. Set aside.

Return the cooled hibiscus tea to the pot and add the remaining ¼ cup sugar. Cook over medium-high heat until reduced to ½ cup, about 15 minutes. Remove from the heat and let cool completely.

When ready to serve, moisten the rim of each glass with a lime wedge and place upside down in the dish containing the powdered hibiscus and sugar mixture. Wiggle the glass to cover the wet part of the rim completely. Divide the cooled hibiscus syrup among the rimmed glasses and top with the chilled sparkling wine. Serve immediately.

White Winter Sangria

IT DOESN'T GET VERY COLD IN SOUTHERN CALI, so sometimes we sip on cold, refreshing cocktails during the winter. Lemongrass grows in abundance in my garden. I often use it to make tea because it helps with digestion, heals colds and flu, and detoxifies and cleanses the body. And it smells amazing. You can make this recipe all year long because you can use pretty much any fruit for this. White peaches in the summer, if they are available to you, would make a lovely variation.

SERVES 4 TO 6

3 stalks lemongrass, coarsely chopped

2 cups water

1 cup granulated sugar

1 (750-ml) bottle semisweet white wine, such as Riesling

1 green apple, cored and diced into ¼-inch cubes

1 cup pomegranate seeds

2 tangerines, sliced into ¼-inch slices

Combine the lemongrass, water, and sugar in a medium saucepan and simmer over medium heat for 15 minutes. Remove from the heat and let steep for 15 minutes. Strain the syrup into a pitcher and let cool. Stir in the wine and fruit. Chill, covered, for at least 1 hour and up to 24 hours. Serve over ice.

Strawberry and Thai Basil Mojito

THE ONLY THING BETTER THAN A MOJITO is this strawberry and Thai basil mojito. This drink relies on the slightly aniselike scent and mildly spicy kick of Thai basil (not present in sweet basil) to make the perfect summer cocktail. You can absolutely use the more common sweet basil, but the subtle licorice flavor from the Thai basil really brings out the flavor of the rum. I often swap out the rum for a reposado tequila or even vodka when I want to keep it extra bright.

SERVES 4

1 cup sliced strawberries, plus 4 left whole, for garnish (optional)

½ cup granulated sugar

¾ cup white rum

4 tablespoons freshly squeezed lime juice (from about 2 limes)

4 tablespoons firmly packed fresh Thai basil

3 cups sparkling water

In a chilled glass, muddle ¼ cup of the strawberries and 2 tablespoons of the sugar. Add 1½ ounces of the rum, 1 tablespoon of the lime juice, and 1 tablespoon of the basil and stir. Fill the glass with ice and top with ¾ cup of the sparkling water. Garnish with whole strawberry, if desired. Repeat with the remaining glasses and serve immediately.

Pear Punch

Calientito de Pera

CALIENTITOS ARE WARMED FRUIT PUNCHES served during the holidays everywhere in Mexico. This is the Casa Marcela version and is absolutely stunning served inside the pears, though that touch is optional if you do not want to bother with hollowing them out, but I guarantee you it is worth it. The smell of the cooked guavas is glorious and makes everyone come to the kitchen to see what's on the stove. Hold off on the tequila if little ones will be enjoying these as well.

SERVES 4 TO 6

4 to 6 red Anjou pears, or any other red pear

Juice of 1 lemon

8 guavas, halved

3½ cups unfiltered apple juice

2 tablespoons brown sugar

1 cinnamon stick, plus 4 to 6 for garnish (optional)

1 star anise, plus 4 to 6 for garnish (optional)

1 (2-inch) strip orange zest, plus 4 to 6 orange slices for garnish (optional)

½ cup tequila reposado

To hollow out the pears, use a melon baller or a spoon, making sure to leave about ¼ inch at the bottom and around the edges to create a cup that will hold liquid. Discard or reserve the pear fruit for other use. Slice the bottom of the pear so it stands on its own. Place on a serving tray. Sprinkle the lemon juice over the pears to prevent browning.

Combine the guava halves, apple juice, brown sugar, cinnamon stick, star anise, and orange peel in a large, heavy pot and bring to a boil over medium-high heat. Decrease the heat and simmer until the flavors infuse, about 20 minutes. Turn off the heat and strain the punch through a fine-mesh strainer into a large, heatproof pitcher. Add the tequila and mix well. Serve the warm punch in the hollowed pears and garnish with a cinnamon stick, star anise, and an orange slice, if desired.

Desserts

Postres

A h … dessert. I was once told that dessert, being the last thing served, is what your dinner will be remembered for, so you'd better make it good. Well, here I deliver plenty of options not only to delight your palate but also entice your mind and heart, to show that what you may have perceived as a very traditional Mexican dessert can now be seen in a new light. Desserts can be somewhat complicated. There's measurements, science, leavening, temperatures, and things that as a savory-foods cook you really don't want to think about, but once you get the hang of it, once you master a few of the techniques, you'll fall in love with the baking process.

In Mexico, most of our desserts are influenced by those of Europe. I found this particularly fabulous while studying classic French pastry at the Ritz Escoffier in Paris (so fancy), because I was able to make a connection between everything I grew up with and the roots of where they actually came from. Even though I have cooked and published many of the classic recipes, in many cases I took some very traditional ingredients or ideas and created something new, because that's what happens at Casa Marcela. We go a little crazy sometimes, but we also love the old-school way of making and serving desserts, so you'll find a little bit of both. What they all have in common is that they will certainly leave your guests and your family with a very delicious memory of an evening at your table, even if your *mole* was a little too bitter.

Mexican Chocolate Cinnamon Rolls with Cream Cheese–Orange Glaze

CINNAMON ROLLS. SOUNDS DAUNTING, HUH? I tried to make the process as easy as possible, and here's the deal—they are so worth it. Mexican chocolate has such a distinct flavor. You can certainly substitute with bittersweet chocolate and add cinnamon, but nothing will get you the robust, unique flavor of true Oaxacan chocolate. The chocolate is still made the same way it has been for centuries—ground with sugar, cinnamon, and almonds. Found in hexagonal or octagonal disks, now in some supermarkets here in the United States and available readily online, it should be a pantry staple. It makes for the most luxurious hot chocolate and is the key and central ingredient in one of Mexico's most representative dishes, mole.

Piloncillo, Mexico's very popular unrefined whole cane sugar, also gives these cinnamon rolls a deeper, richer flavor because of its molasses-like quality. Read more about it on page 180, as it is also used in savory dishes!

MAKES 14 CINNAMON ROLLS

ROLLS

1 cup whole milk

7 tablespoons unsalted butter, at room temperature

3½ cups all-purpose flour, plus more for kneading

½ cup granulated sugar

1 large egg

2¼ teaspoons (1 packet) rapid rise yeast

1¼ teaspoons salt

1 (7½-ounce) piloncillo cone, finely grated

¼ cup finely grated Mexican chocolate

2 tablespoons plus 1 teaspoon ground cinnamon

½ cup chopped pecans

GLAZE

4 ounces cream cheese, at room temperature

4 tablespoons (½ stick) unsalted butter, at room temperature

1 cup sifted powdered sugar

½ teaspoon pure vanilla extract

½ teaspoon grated orange zest

For the rolls, combine the milk and 3 tablespoons of the butter in a bowl and microwave on high until the butter melts and the mixture is just warmed to 120°F to 130°F. Pour the mixture into the bowl of a stand mixer fitted with the paddle attachment. Add 1 cup of the flour, the granulated sugar, egg, yeast, and 1 teaspoon of the salt. Beat on low speed for 3 minutes. Add the remaining 2½ cups flour and beat on low speed until the flour is absorbed and the dough is sticky, scraping down the sides of the bowl as needed. Turn the dough out onto a lightly floured surface. Knead until smooth and elastic, adding more flour as needed, about 9 minutes. Form into a ball, transfer to an oiled medium bowl, and cover with plastic wrap. Let the dough rest at room temperature for 1 hour. (The dough won't double in size, but may look slightly puffy.)

Meanwhile, combine the grated piloncillo, grated chocolate, cinnamon, and remaining ¼ teaspoon salt.

Lightly flour a work surface and scrape the dough out of the bowl and gently roll flat, using a floured rolling pin, into an 8 × 29-inch rectangle. Dot the remaining 4 tablespoons butter all over the surface and sprinkle with the Mexican chocolate mixture and the chopped pecans. Grease a 13 × 9-inch glass baking pan. Set aside.

Starting at one of the 29-inch-long edges, roll up the dough, jelly-roll style. After rolling, push and gently squeeze the roll together to make it 8 inches wide × 29 inches long. Using a sharp knife, cut the roll into fourteen 2-inch-thick slices. Place in the prepared baking pan, with the swirly side facing up, and cover with plastic. Let rise until almost doubled in size, about 1 hour.

Preheat the oven to 375°F. Bake for 25 to 30 minutes, or until golden.

For the glaze, in the bowl of a stand mixer fitted with the paddle attachment, beat the cream cheese and butter until fluffy, about 4 minutes. Add the powdered sugar, vanilla, and orange zest and continue to mix until smooth.

Top each cinnamon roll with a tablespoon of glaze while the rolls are still warm.

Churro Cupcakes

AN EASY RECIPE THAT COMBINES two of my childhood favorites, this is a mashup of epic proportions, because there might be nothing better in the world than churros and cupcakes. My mom made cupcakes from boxed cake mix on the regular. Often they'd be breakfast before school. I used to cross the international border every day to go to school in San Diego, and you know what my mom would get us as a treat for waking up at 5:30 in the morning? A warm, brown bag of churros that would leave our homework papers drenched in grease and our uniforms sprinkled with sugar. Perfection.

MAKES 12 CUPCAKES

CUPCAKES

1¼ cups all-purpose flour

1 teaspoon ground cinnamon

½ teaspoon baking soda

½ teaspoon baking powder

½ teaspoon salt

8 tablespoons (1 stick) unsalted butter, melted

½ cup granulated sugar

½ cup packed light brown sugar

¼ cup sour cream

2 large eggs

1½ teaspoons pure vanilla extract

BUTTERCREAM

6 tablespoons (¾ stick) unsalted butter, at room temperature

1½ teaspoons pure vanilla extract

1 teaspoon ground cinnamon

3 cups powdered sugar, sifted

1½ tablespoons whole milk

CHURRO GARNISH

¼ cup granulated sugar

½ teaspoon ground cinnamon

Vegetable oil, for frying

2 flour tortillas

Preheat the oven to 350°F. Line a standard 12-cup muffin tin with paper liners.

For the cupcakes, in a medium bowl, combine the flour, cinnamon, baking soda, baking powder, and salt. Set aside.

In the bowl of a stand mixer fitted with the paddle attachment, beat the butter, granulated sugar, light brown sugar, sour cream, eggs, and vanilla until fluffy, about 3 minutes. Turn down the speed to low and add the flour mixture. Blend until well combined, about 25 seconds.

Pour about 2½ tablespoons of the batter into each cupcake liner. Bake the cupcakes for 20 minutes, or until a tester inserted into the center comes out clean. Turn the cupcakes out of the pan and let cool on a wire rack.

For the buttercream, in the clean bowl of a stand mixer fitted with the paddle attachment, beat the butter, vanilla, and cinnamon until smooth, about 2 minutes, scraping down the sides as needed. With the machine running on low speed, add the powdered sugar, 1 cup at a time, alternating with the milk. Prepare a pastry bag fitted with a star tip and fill with the buttercream.

For the churro garnish, mix the sugar and cinnamon together on a large plate. Set aside.

In a heavy medium saucepan, add enough oil to come halfway up the sides of the pan. Heat over medium-high heat until a deep-fry thermometer inserted into the oil reaches 350°F. (If you do not have a thermometer, test the oil with a piece of tortilla, which should sizzle when it touches the oil and brown in 2 to 3 minutes.) Meanwhile, place the tortillas on a work surface and, using a cookie cutter, cut the tortilla into different shapes and/or letters. Fry the tortilla shapes until golden brown. With a slotted spoon, transfer the crisps to paper towels to drain. While still warm, transfer to the cinnamon-sugar mixture and turn to coat.

To assemble the cupcakes, make a swirl of buttercream on each cupcake and top with a tortilla crisp.

Dulce de Leche–Stuffed Pastries

Coyotas

I USED TO VISIT MY FAVORITE RESTAURANT IN TIJUANA, El Rodeo, so much that it shouldn't be a surprise that many of my recipes are inspired by them and their Sonoran menu. I had to test these a few times because the texture of the pastry needs to be a perfect mix of flaky (not crumbly), delicate, and flavorful.

MAKES 8

½ cup water

1 (7½-ounce) piloncillo cone (see page 232), shredded

1 tablespoon instant dry yeast

3½ cups all-purpose flour

½ teaspoon salt

¾ cup lard

½ cup dulce de leche

In a small, heavy saucepan over medium heat, combine the water and shredded piloncillo and heat until the piloncillo is completely dissolved. Let the mixture cool until it reaches 110°F. Add the yeast to the warm piloncillo syrup and let sit for 2 minutes, or until the mixture starts to bubble.

Meanwhile, combine the flour and salt in a large bowl. Add the lard and work into the flour until it resembles a coarse meal. Slowly add the cooled piloncillo syrup and mix until moist. Knead for 3 minutes, until smooth; there is no need to dust the counter with flour as the kneading can be done directly in the bowl. Cover with plastic wrap and let rest for 30 minutes.

Divide the dough into sixteen 2½-inch balls. Flatten each ball and roll out to approximately 7 inches in diameter.

Add 1 tablespoon of the dulce de leche in the center of eight of the disks and cover with a second disk of dough, pressing down the sides with a fork and cutting out any excess dough. Score each coyota diagonally, leaving ½ inch in between each slit.

Preheat a large nonstick skillet over medium heat. Add the coyotas and cook until golden brown, about 1½ minutes per side. Serve warm or at room temperature.

Apple Pie

WAIT, WHAT? PIE? YES, PIE. This is reflective of me having grown up so close to the U.S. border that we'd often cross that very border to go on Christmas ornament– and pie-shopping frenzies in Julian, California. If you master this piecrust, it's a huge step toward mastering a lot of dough-making techniques. It's about self-confidence just as much as it is about temperature control (make sure the butter stays cold). Top it off with a huge scoop of vanilla ice cream, preferably while still warm.

SERVES 10 TO 12

CRUST

2½ cups all-purpose flour

2 tablespoons superfine sugar

1 teaspoon salt

½ pound (2 sticks) cold unsalted butter, cut into ¼-inch cubes

6 tablespoons ice water

FILLING

8 Granny Smith apples, cut into ¼-inch wedges (about 10 cups)

1 tablespoon apple cider vinegar

⅔ cup granulated sugar

¼ cup cornstarch

1 teaspoon ground cinnamon

1 large egg, beaten

Vanilla ice cream, for serving

For the crust, in a food processor, pulse the flour, superfine sugar, and salt to combine. Add the butter and pulse until coarse, pea-size crumbs form, about 10 seconds. Transfer the dough to a large bowl and knead, using a silicone spatula, adding the ice water 1 tablespoon at a time until the dough just holds together, making sure not to overwork the dough.

Divide the dough in half and roll each half into a ball. Flatten each ball into a disk with smooth edges, cover with plastic wrap, and refrigerate for at least 2 hours or up to overnight.

On a lightly floured surface, roll out one disk of dough into a 13-inch round. Roll the dough loosely around the rolling pin, and then unfurl it into a 10-inch pie dish. Gently lift and settle the dough into the pan. Trim the excess dough using scissors, leaving a ½-inch overhang, and transfer to the refrigerator.

Roll out the remaining piece of dough on a lightly floured surface with a lightly floured rolling pin into a 16 × 11-inch rectangle. Cut the dough crosswise into eleven 1¼-inch-wide strips. Refrigerate the strips.

Preheat the oven to 350°F.

For the filling, bring 9 cups of water to a boil in a large, heavy pot. Place the apple wedges in a large bowl and pour the boiling water over them. Let rest for 10 minutes, drain, and dry the apples with paper towels. Transfer to a bowl and toss with the vinegar.

Combine the sugar, cornstarch, and cinnamon in a separate bowl, add to the apples, and toss until fully coated.

Fill the pie with the coated apples. Weave a tight lattice pattern over the pie with the pastry strips. Trim all the strips flush with the edge of the pie plate. Fold the bottom crust up over edge of the lattice and crimp. Brush the lattice with the beaten egg.

Bake for 45 to 50 minutes, until the crust is golden and the filling is bubbling. Let the pie cool slightly and serve. Serve with vanilla ice cream.

Coffee Candy Meringues

THESE ARE THE "CRACK" OF MERINGUES. They just are. I lived it. For two days I had these for breakfast, lunch, and dinner. For the coffee candy, look for hard candy that has a little bit of chew to it and is dark in color. Once chopped, it mixes perfectly into the meringue and melts only slightly to release some flavor but not so much that you don't get a coffee-crunch surprise in every bite.

For the Mexican chocolate, even though it is sold ground, I prefer to buy the whole disk and grate it on the fine side of a grater; that way, you get more texture and slightly bigger pieces of chocolate.

SERVES 6 TO 8

25 pieces coffee candy

4 large egg whites, at room temperature

¼ teaspoon salt

1 cup plus 2 tablespoons superfine sugar

2 teaspoons distilled white vinegar

1 teaspoon cornstarch

1 teaspoon pure vanilla extract

1¼ cups heavy cream

2 tablespoons ground Mexican chocolate (see headnote)

Preheat the oven to 300°F. Line a baking sheet with parchment paper.

Place the coffee candy in a food processor and pulse until fine. Set aside.

Combine the egg whites and salt in the bowl of a stand mixer fitted with the whisk attachment and beat on medium speed until they hold soft peaks. Add 1 cup of the superfine sugar, increase the speed to medium-high, and beat until glossy and firm peaks form, about 2 minutes longer. Add the vinegar, cornstarch, and vanilla and beat on high speed for 10 seconds more. Using a plastic spatula, fold in the coffee candy.

Spoon the meringue into a pastry bag and pipe 1½-inch rounds onto the prepared baking sheet, spacing them 1 inch apart. Transfer the baking sheet to the oven and immediately decrease the oven temperature to 250°F. Bake for 1 hour and 15 minutes.

Turn off the heat and let the meringues cool completely in the oven.

Meanwhile, in the bowl of a stand mixer fitted with the whisk attachment, combine the cream and remaining 2 tablespoons sugar and beat on medium speed until firm peaks form, about 3 minutes. Transfer the whipped cream to a bowl for serving.

Top the whipped cream with the ground Mexican chocolate and serve with the coffee meringues.

Churros

I'VE PUBLISHED RECIPES FOR CHURROS BEFORE but have untraditionally added eggs to the batter, more like how you would make a choux pastry. Here I go more traditional, with pretty much just butter, flour, and seasonings. Invest in a good high-temperature thermometer because having a consistent oil temperature will ensure your churros are evenly cooked. There is nothing worse than churros that are golden on the outside but raw on the inside.

MAKES 18 CHURROS

1⅓ cups water

1 tablespoon unsalted butter

1 teaspoon salt

1⅓ cups all-purpose flour

¼ cup granulated sugar

½ teaspoon ground cinnamon

Vegetable oil, for frying

Line a baking sheet with parchment paper.

Combine the water, butter, and salt in a large, heavy pot and bring to a boil. Remove from the heat, add the flour, and mix with a wooden spatula until combined. Let the dough sit until cool enough to handle, about 5 minutes. Knead the dough until smooth, about 1 minute.

Place half of the dough in a piping bag fitted with a large open star tip. Pipe 4-inch-long churros onto the prepared baking sheet. Repeat with the remaining dough.

Combine the sugar and cinnamon on a large platter. Set aside.

Meanwhile, heat 4 to 5 inches of vegetable oil in a large Dutch oven until it registers 365°F on a deep-fry thermometer. Add the churros in batches of three and fry, flipping once, until deep golden brown all over, about 4 minutes. Using a slotted spoon, transfer the churros to a paper towel–lined baking sheet to drain.

Roll the churros in the cinnamon-sugar mixture. Serve immediately.

Calabaza en Tacha Cheesecake

MARIA CRACKERS, Mexico's version of the English tea biscuit, give this cheesecake its buttery, crumbly crust. I adore graham crackers, which you can easily use as a substitute, but to me, the Maria crackers taste like home.

For the ground piloncillo, purchase the cone and grate it on the fine side of a box grater. The moisture content of the sugar cone (it varies) will determine how easy (or not) it is to grate it. You might need to throw some muscle into it!

SERVES 6 TO 8

CHEESECAKE

2½ cups peeled and cubed butternut squash

¾ cup packed shredded piloncillo (see headnote) (from about 3 ounces)

¼ cup water

1 (5-ounce) package Maria crackers, or about 32 graham crackers

8 tablespoons (1 stick) unsalted butter, chilled and cubed

2 (8-ounce) packages cream cheese, at room temperature

½ cup mascarpone, at room temperature

½ cup packed light brown sugar

2 large eggs, at room temperature, lightly beaten

1 teaspoon pure vanilla extract

½ teaspoon ground cinnamon

BRITTLE

¼ cup granulated sugar

4 tablespoons (½ stick) unsalted butter

1 cup toasted and shelled butternut squash seeds (from the butternut squash used for the cheesecake)

½ teaspoon salt

½ teaspoon baking soda

WHIPPED CREAM

½ cup heavy cream

1 tablespoon granulated sugar

For the cheesecake, place the cubed butternut squash, ½ cup of the piloncillo, and the water in a large, heavy pot and bring to a boil over medium-high heat. Decrease the heat, cover, and simmer until the squash is cooked through and caramelized, about 30 minutes. Using a slotted spoon, transfer the squash and ¼ cup of the cooking liquid (the cooking liquid is now the syrup) to a blender and process until very smooth, about 2 minutes; this makes a butternut squash puree. Set aside and let cool, reserving another ⅓ cup of the cooking liquid/syrup for the brittle.

Preheat the oven to 350°F. Butter a 9-inch springform pan.

Blend the Maria crackers and the remaining ¼ cup piloncillo in a food processor until coarse crumbs form. Add the cubed butter and process until the crumbs come together. Press the crumbs into the prepared pan. Bake until the crust is golden brown, about 10 minutes. Cool completely on a wire rack.

In the bowl of a stand mixer fitted with the paddle attachment, beat the cream cheese and mascarpone until creamy, about 1 minute. Add the brown sugar, eggs, vanilla, cinnamon, and ⅓ cup of the butternut squash puree and beat well, scraping down the bowl as needed, until well combined, about 1 minute.

Pour the mixture over the cooled crust and bake until golden brown and the center barely jiggles, about 1 hour. Let cool at room temperature for 2 hours. Cover loosely with plastic wrap, and refrigerate until completely cooled, preferably overnight or for at least 6 hours.

For the brittle, line a baking sheet with parchment paper. Combine the reserved ⅓ cup cooking liquid/syrup, granulated sugar, and butter in a medium stainless steel or other nonreactive pot, and cook until the mixture has thickened, darkened slightly, and reached 300°F on a candy or instant-read thermometer. Remove from the heat. Add the squash seeds, salt, and baking soda and stir until well combined. Quickly pour the caramel onto the prepared baking sheet and let stand until the candy hardens and cools. Break into small pieces.

Once the cheesecake has cooled, release the sides of the springform pan and place on a cake platter.

For the whipped cream, in the bowl of a stand mixer fitted with the whisk attachment, combine the cream and granulated sugar. Beat on medium speed until soft peaks form, about 3 minutes. Place the whipped cream in a pastry bag fitted with a large open star tip. Pipe rosettes around the edge of the cheesecake and top with pieces of the brittle.

Crepas de Cajeta

AH, THE *CREPAS DE CAJETA* MADE TABLESIDE at the Campestre Tijuana
Country Club take me back to a very happy time and place. We'd often wait for
my dad in the restaurant on the weekends while he finished his round of golf, and
this was always the dessert of choice. I read somewhere that this dish was a good
representation of the combination of European technique (the crepe) with native,
Mexican ingredients (*cajeta*), as happens often with desserts of Mexico.
Cajeta, caramel made out of goat's milk, is now easily available, but it can be replaced
with any caramel. I just like *cajeta* better because it's less cloying and perfect for
someone like me who is not fond of very sweet desserts.

MAKES 8 TO 10 CREPES

CREPES

1 cup all-purpose flour

½ cup whole milk

3 large eggs

2 tablespoons granulated sugar

2 tablespoons unsalted butter,
melted, plus more for brushing

Pinch of salt

SAUCE

½ cup cajeta

⅓ cup whole milk

½ cup chopped hazelnuts

Cinnamon Ice Cream
(recipe follows), for serving

For the crepes, combine the flour, milk, eggs, sugar, butter, and salt in a
blender and process until smooth. With a rubber spatula, scrape down
the sides and process for 20 seconds longer. Transfer the batter to a bowl
and let stand, covered, for 1 hour. The batter may be made 1 day in advance and kept covered and chilled.

Heat a 6- to 7-inch crepe pan or nonstick skillet over medium heat
until it is hot. Brush the pan lightly with butter and heat until the pan
is hot but not smoking. Stir the batter and pour ¼ cup of the batter into
the pan. Tilt and rotate the pan quickly to cover the bottom with a layer
of batter. Loosen the edge of the crepe with a spatula, and cook the crepe
until the top appears almost dry, about 1 minute. Flip the crepe and
cook the other side lightly. Fold the crepe in half and then in half again
to form a triangle. Transfer the folded crepe to a plate. Repeat with the
remaining batter, brushing the pan lightly with butter as necessary.

For the sauce, combine the cajeta and milk in a large, heavy sauté pan.
Bring to a boil, lower the heat, and add the folded crepes. Make sure the
crepes are completely coated with the cajeta sauce. Transfer to a platter
and top with the chopped hazelnuts. Serve with the ice cream.

Cinnamon Ice Cream

TAKE THREE INGREDIENTS, MIX THEM TOGETHER, and make ice cream. Done. I don't know about you, but nothing compares to the flavor of sweetened condensed milk. It's a little too sweet for my taste buds, but when frozen and mellowed with whipped cream and seasoned with cinnamon, it not only adds flavor but also gives you that silky texture that makes this treat so special. I've added a couple of variations, but you can really mix in anything you want: Oreos and strawberries, apricots and chopped candied pecans . . . In fact, head to social media and tag me with your inventions, @chefmarcela!

SERVES 4 TO 6

1 (14-ounce) can sweetened condensed milk

5 tablespoons ground cinnamon

2 cups heavy cream

Combine the condensed milk and cinnamon in a medium bowl. Set aside.

Whip the heavy cream in a medium bowl until stiff peaks form. Gently fold the whipped cream into the condensed milk–cinnamon mixture. Transfer to a 9 × 13-inch glass baking dish and cover with plastic. Freeze without stirring at all until firm, at least 6 hours or overnight.

VARIATIONS:

Maria Crackers Ice Cream: Instead of adding cinnamon, add ½ cup crumbled Maria crackers before freezing the mixture.

Mexican Chocolate Ice Cream with Chipotle-Pecan Candied Popcorn: Add ½ cup minced Mexican chocolate to the condensed milk. Serve with Chipotle-Pecan Candied Popcorn (page 245).

Strawberry-Layered Tres Leches Cake

YOU CAN FIND *FRESAS CON CREMA* in every *frutería* around Mexico. It is simply layers of strawberries and sweet cream, sometimes whipped cream, and a drizzle of sweetened condensed milk in a plastic cup, and you eat it with a spoon. Simplest dessert ever! Here I decided to combine two classics by layering this tres leches cake and giving it a much fancier presentation. It really needs to soak overnight to get milky!

Now look at the gorgeous photo. The traditional way you usually see a tres leches cake presented is in a foil baking dish, which is not very appealing to the eye. I turned to the magic of social media, where I have to give credit to whomever has a picture of the layer cake on Pinterest with the edible flowers (there are actually a few). The point is, don't limit yourself to the traditional presentations and ingredients. I routinely look for up to ten different versions of a dish to see what other cooks are doing, and then I develop my own. Social media is a wonderful thing, especially when you are looking for ideas and tips on presenting a luscious dessert or setting a beautiful table.

SERVES 10 TO 12

2 cups all-purpose flour

2 tablespoons baking powder

6 large eggs, separated

1½ cups granulated sugar

1 tablespoon pure vanilla extract

1½ cups whole milk

1 (14-ounce) can sweetened condensed milk

1 (12-ounce) can evaporated milk

2 cups heavy cream

2 cups sliced strawberries

Edible flowers, for decorating (optional)

Preheat the oven to 350°F. Coat two 9-inch round cake pans with non-stick cooking spray.

In a bowl, sift together the flour and baking powder. Set the dry ingredients aside.

In the bowl of a stand mixer fitted with the whisk attachment, whisk the egg whites on medium speed until stiff peaks form, 5 to 6 minutes. With the mixer running slowly, add 1 cup of the sugar and mix until combined. Add the egg yolks, one by one, beating well after each addition. Add the vanilla and mix well to incorporate. Add ½ cup total of the whole milk, alternating with the flour mixture in three additions, starting with the milk and ending with the flour, blending well after each addition.

Divide the batter evenly between the prepared cake pans and bake until golden and a cake tester inserted into the middle comes out clean, 18 to 20 minutes. Remove from the oven, transfer to a wire rack, and let cool in the pan for 20 minutes. Run a knife around the edge and invert the cake layers onto a wire rack. Let cool completely.

Meanwhile, combine the remaining 1 cup whole milk, condensed milk, and evaporated milk in a blender and process until smooth. Refrigerate until ready to use.

Combine the heavy cream and remaining ½ cup sugar in a medium bowl. Using an electric mixer, beat the cream until soft peaks form. Set aside.

Once the cake is completely cooled, using a serrated knife, cut a small portion from the top of each cake to completely flatten it. (Save the trimmings for another use.) Using a fork, poke the top of both cake halves all over. Place the first cake layer on a platter and slowly pour half of the milk mixture on top, making sure it gets completely absorbed. Spread 1 cup of the whipped cream on top, then top with the sliced strawberries. Top with the second cake layer and pour the remaining milk mixture on top, making sure it gets absorbed. Spread the remaining whipped cream over the top and around the sides, pushing the spatula in a forward motion to remove any excess whipped cream. Make sure you don't cover the cake completely, because you want to see some cake behind the cream. Refrigerate overnight before serving.

Decorate the cake with edible flowers, if desired.

Chocolate-Cajeta Brownie Pudding

I REALLY WANTED TO MAKE A BROWNIE WITH *CAJETA*, but my first attempts
were coming out too dry, so I thought, let's do it in a skillet, make it all gooey and
fudgy, and call it a pudding to serve with a spoon. So this happened. Plop it in
the center of the dinner table after you're done with your tacos, top it off with
a big scoop of vanilla ice cream, and just pass around the spoons.

SERVES 8

1 cup semisweet chocolate chips

12 tablespoons (1½ sticks)
plus 2 teaspoons unsalted butter

3 large eggs

1 cup granulated sugar

1 teaspoon pure vanilla extract

1 cup all-purpose flour

1 teaspoon baking powder

¼ teaspoon salt

2 ounces bittersweet chocolate,
cut into chunks

½ cup plus 2 tablespoons cajeta

1 cup vanilla ice cream

Position the rack in the middle of the oven and preheat the oven to 350°F.

Melt the semisweet chocolate and 12 tablespoons of the butter in a
medium heatproof bowl set over a saucepan of simmering water, stirring
occasionally, until smooth. Remove from the heat and let cool slightly.

In the bowl of a stand mixer fitted with the whisk attachment, beat
the eggs and sugar on medium-high speed until creamed, about 3
minutes. Add the vanilla. Pour in the chocolate mixture and whisk until
well combined. Incorporate the flour, baking powder, and salt and mix
for about 2 minutes on medium speed. Stir in the bittersweet chocolate
chunks by hand.

Grease the bottom of a 12-inch cast-iron skillet with the remaining
2 teaspoons butter. Pour in half of the chocolate batter and drizzle with
½ cup of the cajeta. Pour the rest of the chocolate batter on top and bake
for 40 to 45 minutes, until the top is shiny.

Serve warm with the remaining 2 tablespoons cajeta and the vanilla
ice cream.

Cheesecake with Pomegranate Sauce

THIS IS A SHOWSTOPPER FOR SURE. Pomegranates are usually reserved for one of Mexico's most traditional dishes, *chiles en nogada*, stuffed poblano chiles topped with a white walnut sauce and sprinkled with fresh pomegranate seeds. The dish contains the colors of the Mexican flag and is served during the month of September, when Mexico's independence is celebrated on September 16. Here I cook the pomegranate juice down into a syrup with the most gorgeous scarlet color to bring out its sweetness while still retaining a slightly crisp, tart bite.

SERVES 10

POMEGRANATE SAUCE

2 cups pomegranate juice

¼ cup granulated sugar

½ cup fresh pomegranate seeds

CHEESECAKE

12 graham crackers

1½ cups sugar

¼ teaspoon salt

5 tablespoons unsalted butter, melted and cooled

4 (8-ounce) packages cream cheese, at room temperature

½ teaspoon pure vanilla extract

4 large eggs

½ cup sour cream

For the pomegranate sauce, combine the pomegranate juice and sugar in a saucepan and cook without stirring over high heat until reduced to ½ cup, about 15 minutes. Divide the reduced syrup between two separate bowls and let cool. Add the pomegranate seeds to one bowl of sauce, stir to combine, and refrigerate until ready to use. Let the remaining sauce sit at room temperature.

Preheat the oven to 350°F. Wrap three layers of aluminum foil around the outside of a 9-inch-diameter springform pan. Butter the pan.

For the cheesecake, combine the graham crackers, ¼ cup of the sugar, and the salt in a food processor and pulse until crumbly. Add the butter and pulse until moistened. Press the crumb mixture evenly onto the bottom and 1½ inches up the sides of the prepared springform pan. Bake just until golden brown, about 15 minutes. Remove from the oven and cool completely on a wire rack.

Decrease the oven temperature to 325°F.

In the bowl of a stand mixer fitted with the paddle attachment, beat the cream cheese on medium speed until fluffy. Add the remaining 1¼ cups sugar and the vanilla and beat until combined. Add the eggs, one at a time, mixing well after each addition. Add the sour cream and mix until smooth, about 35 seconds. Pour the filling into the cooled crust.

Set the cheesecake in a large baking pan. Add enough hot water to the baking pan to come 1 inch up the sides of the cheesecake pan. Carefully transfer to the oven and bake until almost set but not puffed and the center moves slightly when the pan is gently shaken, about 1 hour. Let cool at room temperature on a wire rack for 2 hours. Pour the reserved syrup without the pomegranate seeds over the cheesecake. Cover loosely with plastic wrap and refrigerate until completely cooled, preferably overnight or for at least 6 hours.

Once the cheesecake has cooled, release and remove the sides of the springform pan, leaving the cake on the bottom of the pan. Place on a cake platter. Pour the reserved ¼ cup syrup with the pomegranate seeds on top of the cooled cheesecake and serve.

Chipotle-Pecan Candied Popcorn

MAKE A BATCH OF THIS and watch it disappear. There's something about that smoky, spicy, and sweet combo that you'll keep coming back for more until the bowl is empty.

SERVES 4

1 cup coarsely chopped pecans

½ cup popcorn kernels, popped and still warm

1 cup packed dark brown sugar

¼ cup honey

4 tablespoons (½ stick) unsalted butter

1 teaspoon salt

1 teaspoon chipotle powder

¼ teaspoon baking soda

Preheat the oven to 250°F. Generously spray a baking sheet with non-stick cooking spray.

Mix the chopped pecans and warm popcorn on the prepared baking sheet. Place in the oven while preparing the syrup.

Combine the brown sugar, honey, and butter in a heavy medium saucepan. Whisk over medium-low heat until the sugar dissolves and the butter is completely melted. Increase the heat to high and boil for 4 minutes, stirring continuously. Remove from the heat. Add the salt, chipotle powder, and baking soda and mix to evenly incorporate. Remove the baking sheet from the oven. Pour the syrup, slowly, over the popcorn-pecan mixture. Stir gently to make sure the popcorn and nuts are completely coated.

Return the baking sheet to the oven and bake until the caramel is dry and has hardened, about 1 hour. Remove from the oven and let cool before serving. The popcorn can be stored in an airtight container for up to 5 days.

Chocolate Cake

JUST A DECADENT CHOCOLATE CAKE, PURE AND SIMPLE. This recipe reminds me of the chocolate cake in the movie *Matilda* (a must if you haven't seen it), and it will bring absolute joy to the chocolate lovers in your life. Chocolate on chocolate on chocolate, as life should be lived.

SERVES 10 TO 12

CAKE

2 cups all-purpose flour

2 cups granulated sugar

¾ cup unsweetened cocoa powder

2 teaspoons baking powder

2 teaspoons baking soda

1 teaspoon salt

1 cup whole milk

1 cup boiling water

½ cup vegetable oil

2 large eggs

1 tablespoon pure vanilla extract

FROSTING

1¾ cups powdered sugar

3 tablespoons unsalted butter

4½ ounces bittersweet chocolate, melted

½ cup sour cream

Preheat the oven to 350°F. Spray two 9-inch round cake pans with non-stick cooking spray.

For the cake, in the bowl of a stand mixer fitted with the paddle attachment, combine the flour, granulated sugar, cocoa powder, baking powder, baking soda, and salt and mix on low speed until well combined and homogeneous in color. With the mixer running on low speed, add the milk, boiling water, vegetable oil, eggs, and vanilla. Mix on high speed for 1 minute, stopping and scraping down the sides as needed, until well combined and the mixture has air bubbles.

Divide the batter between the prepared cake pans and bake for about 40 minutes, until a cake tester inserted into the center comes out clean. Let cool. Run a thin knife around edge of each cake, then invert onto racks and cool completely.

Using a serrated knife, cut a small portion from the top of each cake layer to completely flatten them. (Save the trimmings for another use.)

For the frosting, combine the powdered sugar and butter in a food processor and pulse until well combined. Add the chocolate and continue to pulse, scraping down the sides as needed. Add the sour cream and process until very smooth, about 1 minute.

Place one cake layer on a platter and spread half of the frosting on top (see Note). Flip the second cake layer on top, making sure the trimmed, flattened side is facing the frosting, and spread the remaining frosting to cover only the top of the cake, leaving the sides without frosting. Serve.

NOTE: The cake needs to be frosted within 20 minutes of the frosting being prepared, more or less, depending on room temperature.

Upside-Down Mango Cake

MY MOM WAS FAMOUS for her upside-down pineapple cake, so I took
her recipe to the tropics and made it with mango and coconut. Soft, tender,
and delicate, it's perfect with a nice cup of tea or a cappuccino.

SERVES 10 TO 12

½ cup packed light brown sugar

12 tablespoons (1½ sticks)
unsalted butter

2 large mangoes, cut into
½-inch slices (about 2 cups)

½ cup sweetened
shredded coconut

2¼ cups all-purpose flour

4 teaspoons baking powder

1 teaspoon salt

1½ cups granulated sugar

3 large eggs

1 teaspoon pure vanilla extract

1¼ cups whole milk

Preheat the oven to 350°F. Butter a 9-inch springform pan.

Combine the brown sugar and 4 tablespoons of the butter in a small saucepan over medium heat and stir constantly until the sugar dissolves and the syrup is bubbling. Bring the mixture to a boil until it turns a light amber color. Remove from the heat immediately and carefully pour into the prepared springform pan. Arrange the mango on top, overlapping the slices. Sprinkle the shredded coconut on top and set aside.

Whisk together the flour, baking powder, and salt in a medium bowl and set aside. In the bowl of a stand mixer fitted with the paddle attachment, beat the remaining 8 tablespoons butter and the granulated sugar on high speed until light and fluffy, about 6 minutes. Add the eggs, one at a time, beating well after each addition. Beat in the vanilla. Add half of the flour mixture and mix at low speed until just combined. Mix in the milk, then add the remaining flour mixture, mixing until just combined.

Gently spoon the batter over the mango slices and spread evenly. Place the springform pan on a baking sheet and transfer to a rack in the middle of the oven. Bake for 1 hour, or until golden brown and a tester inserted into the center comes out clean.

Cool the cake in the pan on a wire rack for 10 minutes. Run a thin knife around the inside edges of the pan, then invert a plate over the pan and invert the cake onto the plate. Cool completely on the plate and serve the cake at room temperature.

Capirotada

THIS IS MEXICO'S VERSION OF BREAD PUDDING, which, I have to confess,
I was never a big fan of. It is meant to use up leftover ingredients and create
a simple dessert. In some parts of Mexico they add cheese to balance out the
sweetness, but I felt it simply needed to be more luxurious, and cheese
wasn't fitting in my plans. I prefer to add milk to it, which is more popular in
northern Mexico, where I am from, but this rendition is all Casa Marcela.

SERVES 6 TO 8

5 cups 1-inch cubes bolillo or
soft baguette

4 tablespoons (½ stick)
unsalted butter, melted,
plus more for the pan

1 (14-ounce) can condensed milk

1 (12-ounce) can evaporated milk

1 cup whole milk

1 cinnamon stick

1 star anise

4 tablespoons sliced almonds

3 tablespoons dark raisins

2 tablespoons shredded
unsweetened coconut

Preheat the oven to 350°F.

Line a baking sheet with parchment paper. Butter a 10-inch pie dish.

Place the bolillo cubes in a medium bowl and toss with the melted
butter. Spread on the prepared baking sheet and bake for 15 minutes, or
until crispy.

Combine the condensed milk, evaporated milk, whole milk, cinnamon stick, and star anise in a medium pot and bring to a boil over
medium-high heat. Decrease the heat to low and simmer for 20 minutes.
Remove and discard the cinnamon stick and star anise.

Add half of the bolillo cubes to the prepared pie dish and pour
2 cups of the milk mixture over. Sprinkle with 2 tablespoons of the sliced
almonds, 1½ tablespoons of the raisins, and 1 tablespoon of the shredded
coconut. Repeat with the remaining bread, milk mixture, raisins, almonds,
and coconut. Let sit at room temperature for 30 minutes so the bread can
absorb the liquid.

Bake the bread pudding until golden brown, about 25 minutes. Serve
warm or at room temperature. (Even cold tastes great!)

Buñuelos with Lavender Piloncillo Syrup

THERE'S REALLY NOTHING COMPARABLE to the smell and taste of a freshly fried *buñuelo* off a street cart in any given town in Mexico. They're crispy, sweet, and crumbly, and known for their labor-intensive process. This is an easier version, because after you stretch them out paper-thin so you can almost see through them, you don't have to wait for them to rest or "dry." You can just fry them. You also don't have to wait for Christmas or New Year's to enjoy them, either. Although they are traditionally made for holiday celebrations, they are absolutely welcome on the dessert table year-round. Broken into bits, they can top a scoop of vanilla ice cream with a drizzle of caramel, or you can stack them with layers of whipped cream and berries for a messy napoleon that's simply divine.

As for the lavender syrup, that's all Casa Marcela. Lavender grows wild in my front yard and adorns pretty much every room in the house. Calming, soothing, and fresh, lavender in small amounts is the perfect counterpoint for ultra-sweet and bold piloncillo, the Mexican sugar cone used to make the syrup. If you don't have the chance to try them from a street vendor in Oaxaca, this is surely the next best thing.

MAKES 18

BUÑUELOS

1⅔ cups all-purpose flour, plus 4 tablespoons for dusting

½ cup plus 1 tablespoon granulated sugar

1 teaspoon baking powder

½ teaspoon salt

1 large egg

1 tablespoon unsalted butter, at room temperature

1 teaspoon pure vanilla extract

½ cup warm water

Vegetable oil, for frying

1 teaspoon ground cinnamon

LAVENDER PILONCILLO SYRUP

10 fresh lavender flowers

1 (7½-ounce) piloncillo cone

1 cup water

Peel of ½ orange (not just the zest)

For the buñuelos, combine the flour, 1 tablespoon of the granulated sugar, the baking powder, and the salt in a large bowl. Make a well in the center of the flour mixture and add the egg, butter, and vanilla. Mix with your hands until a coarse meal is formed, turn out of the bowl, and knead on a floured surface with some of the remaining flour, adding 1 tablespoon of the warm water at a time to fully incorporate. Knead until elastic and smooth, about 5 minutes. Place in a flour-dusted bowl and cover with plastic wrap. Let the dough rest for 30 minutes.

Meanwhile, for the lavender syrup, in a heavy saucepan, combine the lavender flowers, piloncillo, and water and bring to a boil over high heat. Once the piloncillo is completely dissolved, decrease the heat to low. Add the orange peel and let infuse over low heat for at least an hour. Strain and cool to room temperature before serving.

In a large, heavy skillet, heat 1 inch of vegetable oil to 365°F on a deep-fry thermometer.

Divide the dough into eighteen 1-tablespoon-size balls and set aside under a damp cloth. On a floured surface, stretch the dough balls one at a time with a rolling pin and roll out each ball to form a circle as thin as possible, without breaking the dough. Place on an inverted bowl covered with a damp towel and pull the edges very gently without breaking. Work slowly and take your time. The buñuelo should be very thin, approximately 6 inches in diameter, and almost transparent. Fry each buñuelo in the oil until golden in color and crisp, about 2 minutes per side. Place on a plate lined with paper towels to drain the excess oil.

Combine the remaining ½ cup granulated sugar and the cinnamon in a small bowl. Sprinkle each buñuelo with the sugar mixture. Stack the buñuelos on a plate and drizzle the lavender syrup on top. Serve at room temperature.

"Azúcar y canela,
hacen a la vida buena."

HOW TO MAKE BUÑUELOS

Divide the dough into eighteen 1-tablespoon-size balls and set aside under a damp cloth.

On a floured surface, stretch the dough balls one by one with a rolling pin and gently roll out each ball to form a circle as thinly as possible without breaking the dough.

Place on an inverted bowl covered with a damp towel and pull the edges very gently without breaking.

Lemon Meringue Pie

THIS IS LIKE A MARGARITA but made into a custard and then into a pie. It's more of a tart, actually. The crust uses my very favorite crust-making cookie: the Maria cracker. For the meringue, make sure you beat the egg whites to stiff peaks; that will make all the difference in being able to pipe beautiful dollops (or rosettes, if you wish). Eggs that are four or five days old make the best meringue. Room-temperature eggs are a must, and meringue hates humidity, so take that into consideration.

SERVES 12

CRUST

1 (5-ounce) package Maria crackers

⅓ cup unsalted butter,
at room temperature

¼ cup sugar

Pinch of salt

FILLING

1 cup granulated sugar

5 tablespoons cornstarch

¼ teaspoon salt

1 cup water

½ cup whole milk

4 large egg yolks (save the whites
for the meringue)

2 teaspoons freshly grated
lemon zest

½ cup freshly squeezed
lemon juice

1 tablespoon unsalted butter

2 teaspoons good-quality
reposado tequila

MERINGUE

6 large egg whites

½ teaspoon cream of tartar

Pinch of salt

1 cup sugar

Preheat the oven to 350°F. Spray a 12-inch tart pan with a removable bottom with nonstick cooking spray.

For the crust, pulse the Maria crackers, butter, sugar, and salt in a food processor until combined. Firmly press the crumb mixture into the prepared tart pan, making sure to come up the sides. Bake for 10 minutes, or until golden brown. Let cool completely on a wire rack. Keep the oven on.

For the filling, in a heavy saucepan over medium-high heat, whisk together the sugar, cornstarch, and salt. Add the water and milk and continue to whisk until the cornstarch is dissolved. Cook, whisking continuously, until the mixture slightly thickens to a custardlike texture. Whisk the egg yolks in a medium bowl and gradually add to the pan. Continue to whisk until combined, and then remove from the heat. Whisk in the lemon zest, lemon juice, and butter. Add the tequila and stir to combine. Cover the filling with plastic wrap and set aside.

For the meringue, in the bowl of a stand mixer fitted with the whisk attachment, beat the egg whites, cream of tartar, and salt on high speed until soft peaks form, 2 to 3 minutes. Reduce the speed to low and gradually add the sugar, continuing to beat until stiff peaks form, another 1 to 2 minutes. Transfer to a pastry bag fitted with a star tip.

Pour the lemon filling into the cooled tart shell and spread to the edges. Pipe peaked dollops of meringue in concentric circles over the filling. Transfer to the oven and bake for about 15 minutes, until the meringue peaks turn light brown. Let cool at room temperature for about 30 minutes. Chill the tart until completely set, about 1 hour, before serving.

INDEX

NOTE: Page references in *italics* indicate photographs.

A

Almonds
    Aztec Fruit Bars, 177
    Capirotada, 248
    Granola, 174–76, *175*
Amaranth
    Aztec Fruit Bars, 177
Apple(s)
    and Chorizo Stuffing, Crown
        Pork Roast with, *104*, 105–6
    Ground Pork Patties in Tomatillo
        Salsa, 86, *87*
    -Mint Lamb Chops, 80–81
    Pie, 227–28
Arugula
    Prosciutto Salad on a Stick, 48
    Squash Blossom Stacked
        Quesadilla, 23–24, *25*
Avocado(s)
    Bean Cream Soup, 64
    Crema, 151
    Mexican Turkey Club Sandwich,
        38, *39*
    Tomatillo Ceviche Tostaditas, 19

B

Baptisms, Mexican, 72
Bars, Aztec Fruit, 177

Basil
    and Corn, White Rice with, *97*,
        128
    Mexican Ramen, 61–63, *62*
    Roasted Salmon and Pesto-
        Stuffed Anaheim Chiles,
        30–31
    Thai, and Strawberry Mojito,
        212, *213*
Bean(s)
    and Chickpea Salad, 59
    Cream Soup, 64
    Massaged Kale–Cilantro Salad,
        57, *57*
    Oxtail, and Chile Stew, 69–71,
        70
    Red Chile and Short Rib Stew,
        65–66
    Refried, Healthy, 129
Beef
    Grilled Steak and Cheese
        Tostadas, 11
    Mexican Ramen, 61–63, *62*
    Oxtail, Bean, and Chile Stew,
        69–71, *70*
    Peppercorn-Crusted Flank Steak
        with Mustard Cream, 99
    Picadillo-Stuffed Jalapeño
        Chiles, *20*, 21–22
    Pounded Fillet Topped with Salsa
        Ranchera, 112

    Prime Rib Roast, *114*, 115–16
    Red Chile and Short Rib Stew,
        65–66
    Strips, Grilled, *100*, 101
    Tongue, Braised, Tacos in Green
        Salsa, 8
Beets, Pickled, *34*, 35
Bizcochuelos with Thyme-Piloncillo
    Butter, 180–81
Breads
    Bizcochuelos with Thyme-
        Piloncillo Butter, 180–81
    Conchas, *182*, 183–84, *185*
    Mantecadas, 186
    Mexican Chocolate Cinnamon
        Rolls with Cream Cheese–
        Orange Glaze, 222–23
Broccoli and Nopales, Roasted,
    135
Brownie Pudding, Chocolate-
    Cajeta, *240*, 241
Brussels Sprouts
    Ensenada-Style Fish Tacos,
        40–41
    Felipe's, 130, *131*
Buñuelos with Lavender Piloncillo
    Syrup, *250*, 251–54,
    253–55
Burritos
    Chorizo and Egg, 167

Grilled Shrimp, with Chile
Peanut Butter, 9
Butter, Thyme-Piloncillo, 180–81

C

Cabbage
Green Hominy and Pork Soup,
67–68
Mexican Ramen, 61–63, 62
Cajeta
-Chocolate Brownie Pudding,
240, 241
Crepas de, 234
Cakes
Chocolate, 246
Strawberry-Layered Tres
Leches, 236, 237–38, 239
Upside-Down Mango, 247
Calabaza en Tacha Cheesecake,
232–33
Capirotada, 248
Cashews
Habanero Crema (nondairy),
150
Cauliflower Steaks, Roasted, with
Pickled-Jalapeño Vinaigrette,
126, 127
Ceviche, Octopus, 4, 5
Cheese
Bean Cream Soup, 64
Breakfast Skillet, 164, 165–66
Calabaza en Tacha Cheesecake,
232–33
Cheesecake with Pomegranate
Sauce, 242–44, 243
Chickpea and Bean Salad, 59
Chipotle and Shredded-
Chicken Chilaquiles, 170,
171–73

Cottage, Fruit Salad with,
174–76, 175
Cream, -Orange Glaze,
Mexican Chocolate
Cinnamon Rolls with,
222–23
Creamed Rajas-Stuffed Chicken
Breast, 95
Creamy Beer Shrimp-Stuffed
Poblano Chiles, 102, 103
and Grilled Steak Tostadas, 11
Kale-Potato Enchiladas Verdes,
118–19
Massaged Kale-Cilantro Salad,
57, 57
Mexican Turkey Club Sandwich,
38, 39
Pomegranate and Chicken
Salad Lettuce Cups, 49
Squash Blossom Stacked
Quesadilla, 23–24, 25
Sweet Potato Enchiladas, 82, 83
Tomatillo Ceviche Tostaditas, 19
Watermelon, Queso Fresco, and
Mint Salad, 58
Cheesecakes
Calabaza en Tacha Cheesecake,
232–33
with Pomegranate Sauce,
242–44, 243
Chicken
Breast, Creamed Rajas-Stuffed,
95
Jalapeño Roasted, 92, 93
and Pomegranate Salad Lettuce
Cups, 49
-Shredded, and Chipotle
Chilaquiles, 170, 171–73
-Shredded, and Chorizo
Tostadas, Spicy, 12–13
Tamales de Pollo en Salsa Verde,
191–97, 193–97

Thighs, Braised, 98
Chickpea(s)
and Bean Salad, 59
Massaged Kale-Cilantro Salad,
57, 57
Chilaquiles, Chipotle and Shredded-
Chicken, 170, 171–73
Chile(s)
Anaheim, Roasted Salmon and
Pesto-Stuffed, 30–31
Chipotle and Shredded-
Chicken Chilaquiles, 170,
171–73
Creamed Rajas-Stuffed Chicken
Breast, 95
Crispy Potato and Poblano
Tacos, 18
de Árbol, Salsa de, 154
de Árbol Peanut Butter, 140
Drunken Salsa with Mezcal, 141
Green Hominy and Pork Soup,
67–68
Habanero Crema (nondairy),
150
Jalapeño, Picadillo-Stuffed, 20,
21–22
Jalapeño Roasted Chicken, 92,
93
Lime and Serrano Cured
Shrimp, 16
Morita, Guajillo, and Pasilla,
Salsa, 148
Onion, and Tomato, Scrambled
Eggs with, 168
Oxtail, and Bean Stew, 69–71,
70
Pickled Poblanos, 155
Pineapple, Morita, and Pine Nut
Salsa, 152
Poblano, Creamy Beer Shrimp-
Stuffed, 102, 103
Poblano Rings, 132, 133

Pork Shoulder in Morita-Hoisin
Sauce, 78–79
Red, and Short Rib Stew, 65–66
Red, –Lamb Stew, 84–85
Roasted-Cauliflower Steaks
with Pickled-Jalapeño
Vinaigrette, *126*, 127
Salsa de Molcajete, 144–47,
145–47
Spicy Shredded-Chicken and
Chorizo Tostadas, 12–13
Chocolate
Aztec Fruit Bars, 177
-Cajeta Brownie Pudding, *240*,
241
Cake, 246
Mexican, Cinnamon Rolls with
Cream Cheese–Orange
Glaze, 222–23
Mexican, Ice Cream with
Chipotle-Pecan Candied
Popcorn, 235
Chorizo
and Apple Stuffing, Crown Pork
Roast with, *104*, 105–6
and Egg Burritos, 167
and Shredded-Chicken
Tostadas, Spicy, 12–13
Churro Cupcakes, 224–25
Churros, 230, *231*
Cilantro
Avocado Crema, 151
Cream, Steamed Mussels in,
26, 27
Green Hominy and Pork Soup,
67–68
-Massaged Kale Salad, 57,
57
Mexican Ramen, 61–63, *62*
and Mint Salsa Verde, 153
Salsa Verde, 118–19, 143

Cinnamon
Ice Cream, 235
Mexican Chocolate Rolls with
Cream Cheese–Orange
Glaze, 222–23
Coconut
Capirotada, 248
Granola, 174–76, *175*
Upside-Down Mango Cake,
247
Cod
Ensenada-Style Fish Tacos,
40–41
Fritters with Chipotle Tartar
Sauce, 32–33
Coffee Candy Meringues, 229
Coke-Braised Pork Tacos, *14*, 15
Conchas, *182*, 183–84, *185*
Corn
and Basil, White Rice with, *97*,
128
Creamed Rajas–Stuffed Chicken
Breast, 95
Red Chile and Short Rib Stew,
65–66
Cracklings
Bean Cream Soup, 64
in Spicy Red Salsa, 10
Cranberries
Aztec Fruit Bars, 177
Granola, 174–76, *175*
Crema
Avocado, 151
Habanero (nondairy), 150
Crepas de Cajeta, 234
Cucumber, Kohlrabi, and Spinach
Salad, *50*, 51–52
Cupcakes, Churro, 224–25

D

Day of the Dead, 43
Desserts
Apple Pie, 227–28
Buñuelos with Lavender
Piloncillo Syrup, *250*,
251–54, *253–55*
Calabaza en Tacha Cheesecake,
232–33
Capirotada, 248
Cheesecake with Pomegranate
Sauce, 242–44, *243*
Chipotle-Pecan Candied
Popcorn, 245
Chocolate-Cajeta Brownie
Pudding, *240*, 241
Chocolate Cake, 246
Churro Cupcakes, 224–25
Churros, 230, *231*
Cinnamon Ice Cream, 235
Coffee Candy Meringues, 229
Crepas de Cajeta, 234
Dulce de Leche–Stuffed
Pastries, 226
Horchata y Kahlúa Granita, 217
Lemon Meringue Pie, 256–57
Maria Crackers Ice Cream, 235
Mexican Chocolate Cinnamon
Rolls with Cream Cheese–
Orange Glaze, 222–23
Mexican Chocolate Ice Cream
with Chipotle-Pecan
Candied Popcorn, 235
Strawberry-Layered Tres
Leches Cake, *236*, 237–
38, *239*
Upside-Down Mango Cake,
247
Drinks
Hibiscus Mimosas, 208, *209*
Horchata y Kahlúa Granita, 217

Mexican Mule, *206*, 207
Pear Punch, *214*, 215
Popcorn Atole, 216
Strawberry and Thai Basil
    Mojito, 212, *213*
White Winter Sangria, 211
Dulce de Leche–Stuffed Pastries, 226

E

Egg(s)
    Breakfast Skillet, *164*, 165–66
    and Chorizo Burritos, 167
    Huitla Waffle, 178, *179*
    Scrambled, with Onion, Tomato,
        and Chile, 168
Empanadas, Tuna, 36
Enchiladas
    Sweet Potato, *82*, 83
    Verdes, Kale-Potato, 118–19

F

Fennel, Zucchini, and Mint Salad, 60
Fish
    Cod Fritters with Chipotle Tartar
        Sauce, 32–33
    Huitla Waffle, 178, *179*
    Roasted Salmon and Pesto-
        Stuffed Anaheim Chiles,
        30–31
    Roasted Tomatillo Salmon, 96,
        97
    Tacos, Ensenada-Style, 40–41
    Tuna Empanadas, 36
    Whole Fried, *88*, 89–90, *91*
Fritters, Cod, with Chipotle Tartar
    Sauce, 32–33
Fruit. *See also specific fruits*
    Bars, Aztec, 177

Salad with Cottage Cheese,
    174–76, *175*
White Winter Sangria, 211

G

Granita, Horchata y Kahlúa, 217
Granola, 174–76, *175*

H

Hazelnuts
    Crepas de Cajeta, 234
    Granola, 174–76, *175*
Hibiscus Mimosas, 208, *209*
Hoisin-Morita Sauce, Pork Shoulder
    in, 78–79
Hominy
    Oxtail, Bean, and Chile Stew,
        69–71, *70*
    and Pork Soup, Green, 67–68
Huitla Waffle, 178, *179*

I

Ice Cream
    Cinnamon, 235
    Maria Crackers, 235
    Mexican Chocolate, with
        Chipotle-Pecan Candied
        Popcorn, 235

K

Kahlúa y Horchata Granita, 217
Kale
    Massaged, -Cilantro Salad, 57,
        57

-Potato Enchiladas Verdes,
    118–19
Kohlrabi, Cucumber, and Spinach
    Salad, *50*, 51–52

L

Lamb
    Chops, Apple-Mint, 80–81
    -Red Chile Stew, 84–85
Lavender Piloncillo Syrup, Buñuelos
    with, *250*, 251–54, *253–55*
Lemon Meringue Pie, 256–57
Lettuce Cups, Pomegranate and
    Chicken Salad, 49
Lime and Serrano Cured Shrimp, 16

M

Mango Cake, Upside-Down, 247
Mantecadas, 186
Maria Crackers Ice Cream, 235
Masa harina
    Pineapple Tamales, 198
    Tamales de Pollo en Salsa Verde,
        191–97, *193–97*
Meat. *See* Beef; Lamb; Pork
Mercado Hidalgo, 156
Meringues, Coffee Candy, 229
Mezcal, Drunken Salsa with, 141
Mint
    -Apple Lamb Chops, 80–81
    and Cilantro Salsa Verde, 153
    Mexican Mule, *206*, 207
Mushroom Gravy, for Prime Rib
    Roast, *114*, 115–16
Mussels, Steamed, in Cilantro
    Cream, 26, *27*

Mustard Cream, Peppercorn-
    Crusted Flank Steak with, 99

N

Noodles. *See* Ramen
Nopales
    Breakfast Skillet, *164*, 165–66
    and Broccoli, Roasted, 135
Nut(s)
    Aztec Fruit Bars, 177
    Capirotada, 248
    Chile de Árbol Peanut Butter, 140
    Chipotle-Pecan Candied
        Popcorn, 245
    Crepas de Cajeta, 234
    Granola, 174–76, *175*
    Habanero Crema (nondairy),
        150
    Mexican Chocolate Cinnamon
        Rolls with Cream Cheese–
        Orange Glaze, 222–23
    Pecan Pesto, 30–31
    Pine, and Pineapple, Morita
        Salsa, 152

O

Oats
    Granola, 174–76, *175*
Octopus Ceviche, *4*, 5
Onions
    Pickled, 30–31
    Red, Pickled, 149

P

Pastries, Dulce de Leche–Stuffed,
    226

Peanut Butter
    Chile, Grilled Shrimp Burritos
        with, 9
    Chile de Árbol, 140
Pear Punch, *214*, 215
Pecan(s)
    -Chipotle Candied Popcorn,
        245
    Mexican Chocolate Cinnamon
        Rolls with Cream Cheese–
        Orange Glaze, 222–23
    Pesto, 30–31
Peppercorn-Crusted Flank Steak
    with Mustard Cream, 99
Pesto and Roasted Salmon–Stuffed
    Anaheim Chiles, 30–31
Picadillo-Stuffed Jalapeño Chiles,
    20, 21–22
Pickled Beets, *34*, 35
Pickled Onions, 30–31
Pickled Poblanos, 155
Pickled Red Onions, 149
Pies
    Apple, 227–28
    Lemon Meringue, 256–57
Pineapple
    Fruit Salad with Cottage
        Cheese, 174–76, *175*
    Morita, and Pine Nut Salsa, 152
    Tacobab al Pastor, 17
    Tamales, 198
Pine Nut, Pineapple, and Morita
    Salsa, 152
Pomegranate
    and Chicken Salad Lettuce
        Cups, 49
    Massaged Kale–Cilantro Salad,
        57, *57*
    Sauce, Cheesecake with, 242–
        44, *243*

Popcorn
    Atole, 216
    Chipotle-Pecan Candied,
        245
Pork. *See also* Chorizo; Cracklings
    Coke-Braised, Tacos, *14*, 15
    Crown Roast, with Chorizo and
        Apple Stuffing, *104*, 105–6
    Ground, Patties in Tomatillo
        Salsa, 86, *87*
    and Hominy Soup, Green,
        67–68
    Prosciutto Salad on a Stick, 48
    Shoulder in Morita-Hoisin
        Sauce, 78–79
    Tacobab al Pastor, 17
Potato(es)
    Breakfast Skillet, *164*, 165–66
    Chorizo and Egg Burritos,
        167
    Jalapeño Roasted Chicken, *92*,
        93
    -Kale Enchiladas Verdes, 118–19
    Pickled Beets, *34*, 35
    and Poblano Tacos, Crispy, 18
    Red Chile and Short Rib Stew,
        65–66
    Sweet, Enchiladas, *82*, 83
Poultry. *See* Chicken; Turkey
Prosciutto Salad on a Stick, 48
Pudding
    Capirotada, 248
    Chocolate-Cajeta Brownie,
        240, 241

Q

Quesadilla, Squash Blossom
    Stacked, 23–24, *25*

R

Radishes
    Cucumber, Kohlrabi, and
        Spinach Salad, *50*, 51–52
    Mexican Ramen, 61–63, *62*
Raisins
    Capirotada, 248
    Granola, 174–76, *175*
    Picadillo-Stuffed Jalapeño
        Chiles, *20*, 21–22
    Pineapple Tamales, 198
Ramen, Mexican, 61–63, *62*
Rice
    Horchata y Kahlúa Granita, 217
    White, with Basil and Corn, *97*,
        128
Rum
    Strawberry and Thai Basil
        Mojito, 212, *213*

S

Salads
    Chickpea and Bean, 59
    Cucumber, Kohlrabi, and
        Spinach, *50*, 51–52
    Fruit, with Cottage Cheese,
        174–76, *175*
    Massaged Kale–Cilantro, *57*, 57
    Pomegranate and Chicken,
        Lettuce Cups, 49
    Prosciutto, on a Stick, 48
    Watermelon, Queso Fresco, and
        Mint, 58
    Zucchini, Fennel, and Mint, 60
Salmon
    Huitla Waffle, 178, *179*
    Roasted, and Pesto-Stuffed
        Anaheim Chiles, 30–31
    Tomatillo, Roasted, 96, *97*

Salsa
    Apple-Mint, 80–81
    de Chile de Árbol, 154
    de Molcajete, 144–47, *145–47*
    Drunken, with Mezcal, 141
    Green, Braised Beef Tongue
        Tacos in, 8
    Morita, Guajillo, and Pasilla
        Chile, 148
    Pineapple, Morita, and Pine Nut,
        152
    Ranchera, Pounded Fillet
        Topped with, 112
    Spicy Red, Cracklings in, 10
    Tomatillo, Ground Pork Patties
        in, 86, *87*
    Verde, 118–19, 142
    Verde, Mint and Cilantro, 153
Salt, 121
Sandwich, Mexican Turkey Club,
    38, *39*
Sauces. *See also* Salsa
    Avocado Crema, 151
    Chipotle Tartar, 32–33
    Habanero Crema (nondairy),
        150
    Pomegranate, 242–44, *243*
Sausages. *See* Chorizo
Seafood. *See also* Fish; Shrimp
    Octopus Ceviche, *4*, 5
    Steamed Mussels in Cilantro
        Cream, *26*, 27
Shrimp
    Creamy Beer, –Stuffed Poblano
        Chiles, 102, *103*
    Grilled, Burritos with Chile
        Peanut Butter, 9
    Lime and Serrano Cured, 16
Small bites
    Braised Beef Tongue Tacos in
        Green Salsa, 8

    Cod Fritters with Chipotle Tartar
        Sauce, 32–33
    Coke-Braised Pork Tacos, *14*, 15
    Cracklings in Spicy Red Salsa,
        10
    Crispy Potato and Poblano
        Tacos, 18
    Ensenada-Style Fish Tacos,
        40–41
    Grilled Shrimp Burritos with
        Chile Peanut Butter, 9
    Grilled Steak and Cheese
        Tostadas, 11
    Lime and Serrano Cured
        Shrimp, 16
    Mexican Turkey Club Sandwich,
        38, *39*
    Octopus Ceviche, *4*, 5
    Picadillo-Stuffed Jalapeño
        Chiles, *20*, 21–22
    Pickled Beets, *34*, 35
    Roasted Salmon and Pesto-
        Stuffed Anaheim Chiles,
        30–31
    Spicy Shredded Chicken and
        Chorizo Tostadas, 12–13
    Squash Blossom Stacked
        Quesadilla, 23–24, *25*
    Steamed Mussels in Cilantro
        Cream, *26*, 27
    Tacobab al Pastor, 17
    Tomatillo Ceviche Tostaditas, 19
    Tuna Empanadas, 36
Soups
    Bean Cream, 64
    Green Hominy and Pork, 67–68
    Mexican Ramen, 61–63, *62*
Spinach, Cucumber, and Kohlrabi
    Salad, *50*, 51–52
Squash
    Blossom Stacked Quesadilla,
        23–24, *25*

Calabaza en Tacha Cheesecake, 232–33
Red Chile and Short Rib Stew, 65–66
Zucchini, Fennel, and Mint Salad, 60

Stews
Oxtail, Bean, and Chile, 69–71, *70*
Red Chile and Short Rib, 65–66
Red Chile–Lamb, 84–85

Strawberry
-Layered Tres Leches Cake, *236*, 237–38, *239*
and Thai Basil Mojito, 212, *213*

Sweet Potato Enchiladas, *82*, 83

T

Tacobab al Pastor, 17

Tacos
Braised Beef Tongue, in Green Salsa, 8
Coke-Braised Pork, *14*, 15
Crispy Potato and Poblano, 18
Fish, Ensenada-Style, 40–41

Tamales
de Pollo en Salsa Verde, 191–97, *193–97*
Pineapple, 198

Tequila
Lemon Meringue Pie, 256–57
Mexican Mule, *206*, 207

Pear Punch, *214*, 215
Thyme-Piloncillo Butter, 180–81, *182*

Tomatillo(s)
Braised Beef Tongue Tacos in Green Salsa, 8
Ceviche Tostaditas, 19
Green Hominy and Pork Soup, 67–68
Salmon, Roasted, 96, *97*
Salsa, Ground Pork Patties in, 86, *87*
Salsa Verde, 118–19, 143
Tamales de Pollo en Salsa Verde, 191–97, *193–97*

Tomato(es)
Breakfast Skillet, *164*, 165–66
Chipotle and Shredded-Chicken Chilaquiles, *170*, 171–73
Cracklings in Spicy Red Salsa, 10
Octopus Ceviche, *4*, 5
Onion, and Chile, Scrambled Eggs with, 168
Picadillo-Stuffed Jalapeño Chiles, *20*, 21–22
Pounded Fillet Topped with Salsa Ranchera, 112
Salsa de Molcajete, 144–47, *145–47*
Tuna Empanadas, 36

Tostadas
Grilled Steak and Cheese, 11

Spicy Shredded-Chicken and Chorizo, 12–13
Tostaditas, Tomatillo Ceviche, 19
Tuna Empanadas, 36

Turkey
Breast, Spicy, *110*, 111
Club Sandwich, Mexican, 38, *39*

V

Vegetables. *See specific vegetables*

W

Waffle, Huitla, 178, *179*
Watermelon, Queso Fresco, and Mint Salad, 58

Wine
Hibiscus Mimosas, 208, *209*
White Winter Sangria, 211

Z

Zucchini
Fennel, and Mint Salad, 60
Red Chile and Short Rib Stew, 65–66
Squash Blossom Stacked Quesadilla, 23–24, *25*